Dot on the Prairie

Wandering Back to Saskatchewan

CeSloan

CHARLOTTE EVELYN SLOAN

ISBN   978-1-7775187-1-4 (Hardcover)
ISBN   978-1-7775187-0-7 (Paperback)
ISBN   978-1-7775187-2-1 (EPUB)
ISBN   987-1-7775187-3-8 (Kindle)

Artwork on cover by Sunny Justice Cooper

Editing & Proofreading Services, Lantern Hill Communications

Published by Marmie's Corner

First Edition: January 2021

CONTENTS

THE DAY EVERYTHING CHANGED FOREVER

June 1955

Will saw the police car first, parked on the side of the road. He stood right up in the buggy and yelled, "Holy cow! Did somebody get shot?"

Roy eased Queenie past the black and white vehicle and slapped the leather lines as she picked up the pace towards our house. We had never seen a cop car on our road before, and we sure weren't expecting anything unusual as we made our way home from school. Nick and I were riding in the back with our legs swinging over the edge. Our two older brothers, Roy and Will, had the best view from the buggy seat. At the house, we saw more cars, and people in the yard.

"Whoa, Queenie!" Roy pulled back on the lines, and our neighbor, Mr. Fiske, stepped up without a word to take the horse's bridle. He unhooked her from the buggy shafts and led her towards the water trough.

Right away, Dad came to us, along with Aunt Hazel. They took us into the house. I didn't see Mom anywhere, or little Mac. Aunt Hazel hardly ever came to visit, as they lived in the city, about thirty miles away. I was wondering, "Why she is here, and where's Mom?"

Aunt Hazel was crying. Her nose was red, and she kept rubbing her eyes with a soaking wet handkerchief. Dad's eyes were small and squinty, and he didn't look at us. I don't remember any of the details, or who said what. They were saying our mom was dead. Dead! She couldn't be! She was fine as anything a few hours ago when she handed us our lunch kits and waved us off to school. Roy asked about the cop car. The answer came from our aunt as she choked out the words, "They're just trying to help us."

My brothers and I escaped to the boys' bedroom upstairs and closed the door. Then we stared at each other, not knowing what to say. The two bedrooms were side by side, and I decided to check Mom and Dad's door to see if she was in there.

I turned the knob and stepped inside. All I could see was the sun shining on the bare mattress with the tufted buttons. There were no blankets or pillows, as there should have been. As I was leaving the room, I noticed a large pile on the floor. Sheets and towels were rolled up in a heap and they were all soaked red with blood.

So, there we were, the four of us, holed up together. Aunt Hazel said our little brother Mac was at the neighbors'. I wished he was here with us. I wanted us all to be together. When I came back into the room, I saw Roy, the oldest, standing at the window, looking down at the cars and people below. I wondered why they didn't go home. If what Dad said was true about Mom, that she was gone and never coming back, then there was nothing they could do for us. Will had his arm around Nick as they sat in the middle of one of the beds.

Never being able to keep anything to myself, I blurted out, "There's blood all over Mom's room." That was an exaggeration, but I said it anyway. Nick burst out sobbing, and Will, always the kindest and best of us, hugged him tighter.

Nick was only five. He had been invited by the teacher to enjoy a few days of school in preparation for starting Grade 1 in the fall. He had been loving the buggy ride, and feeling like a big boy attending school for the past couple of days. At this moment, he looked like a crumpled up toddler, hiding his face in Will's shirt.

Will was the one who could smooth out a fight, and was the only one Dad didn't yell at. He seemed older than twelve. He motioned to me.

"Dot, give me a blanket, Nicky's shaking." I grabbed the quilt off the other bed, and tucked it around them both. How long we stayed there, I don't know. All questions and no answers. Finally, Mac came in smiling. I knew he had no clue. And so began our days as a motherless family.

THAT FIRST SUMMER WITHOUT MOM

Aunt Hazel stayed at our house for two weeks. How I wished she would talk to us about Mom, about anything. She cried most of the time. It made us feel like crying, too. Even though she was my Mom's younger sister, we didn't know her well. Aunt Hazel lived in Stillwater, a city thirty miles away, and they seldom came to visit. She and Mom wrote letters, but probably my aunt was wishing now that she had spent more time with Mom when she had the chance.

I don't remember a funeral, which is strange, because I have an excellent memory for details. There must have been a funeral. That time in my life is blocked out of my mind. I remember though, that Aunt Hazel was kind to us. We stayed home from school for a while, and then we went back for the last few days of the school year. She helped us get ready in the mornings, cooked breakfast, and sent first-rate lunches with us. Nick stuck to us like glue. I thought he might want to stay home with our aunt and Mac, but he ran and got in the buggy, shaking his head when we told him he could stay home.

It was a bright and sunny June morning, the first day we went back to our one-room school. Queenie briskly trotted along, as the buggy was light, and she was a good puller. Nick and I watched the buggy wheel tracks in the sand, as we looked down the road behind us. The leaves still had that "spring green" color, and grass was starting to grow up in the ditches. Everything was the same, but everything was different. Life would never be the same again because of *that Day*, the one that changed everything.

Back at school, I heard two girls from my grade talking at recess.

"Why did her mom die?"

"I don't know, you ask her."

"No, you…"

I hoped they didn't ask, because I didn't know the answer. As I left the school on the final day of the year, I said to myself, "I'm ten years old. I have just passed into Grade 5. And I don't have a mother."

Summer holidays came, and so did old Aunt Min. She was Dad's aunt, which made her our great aunt, but there was nothing *great* about her. Some of the relatives suggested she would be a help to us, and so she moved in. As it turned out, she was looking for a free place to stay. Day after day, she parked herself in the rocking chair, with her yappy little dog, Trixie, on her lap. Like a queen on her throne, she ordered us kids around. She'd point her cane at whichever kid was closest.

"Peel those spuds and get crackin'!"

"We need wood. Now move it!"

We giggled when we heard her muttering to herself, "Where's that biggest boy? Useless brat!" We could hardly wait to tell Roy.

When we heard she was coming, the boys were excited about having a house dog to play with, but they forgot that in a hurry. She forbade anyone to touch the dog. We didn't want to touch him either, once we got a look at his crusty red-rimmed eyes and missing teeth.

When she came, Aunt Min brought some food that smelled bad. Thankfully, she wasn't about to share it with us. One day, she lost her false teeth, and sent out a call for us to find them. I was the lucky one. I found them in a glass on the bedroom window sill. The pale pink gums, and the fake, white teeth looked hideous floating in the water. She was a mean one, even mean to our little brother Mac, the baby of the family. We were all trying to care for him now that Mom was gone. His proper name was Martin Allan Cleaver, but right from the day he came home from the hospital as a newborn, we called him Mac. Mom had planned for that, if he was a boy, to use the first letter of each name. MAC.

Towards the end of Aunt Min's stay with us, Mac spilled his glass of milk on the table. She was fast. She grabbed her cane and reached across the table to poke him with it. Will was fast, too. He shot out of his seat behind the table, grabbed her cane by the rubber tip and pushed it back at her, while Nick ran to tell Dad. I think Dad had already caught on that she wasn't there to help us at all, and one thing Dad certainly didn't need was another person to look after. When he loaded her up in the truck, we were standing by the house clapping and cheering as they left the yard. All together we punched the air above us three times as we yelled out, "Hip-hip Hooray! Hip-hip Hooray! Hip-hip Hooray!" Nick and Mac were so happy, they threw grass and dirt in the air. They didn't care that it came down on their heads!

OUR FIRST HOUSEKEEPER

July 1955

After Aunt Min's unwelcome visit, Dad hired Mrs. Wheeler. We didn't like her, but she was an experienced cook, and she did a lot of work. She was bossy with us, but we expected that, as we were already used to doing lots of chores. There was always kitchen clean-up and dishes to wash, wood and water to carry, chickens to feed, and a thousand other jobs. Even Nick kept busy most of the day, the same as the rest of us. Only little Mac got off scot-free.

I wonder how we looked through Mrs. Wheeler's eyes as she stepped into our lives that summer. Roy was 14, "on the grow", with a big appetite. He had slightly curly hair, and a crooked grin. He probably would be a mechanic when he grew up, always tinkering with something, or helping to get the old truck going. Will was 12, with brown eyes and dark hair like Mom. Give him a few more years, and he would be the "looker" of the family. Then, it was me, ten years old, and being the only girl was my claim to fame. I think I had ordinary looks, straight brown hair, and blue eyes like the Grandma Dot I was named after. Nick was next, five years old and cute as a button, with a smattering of freckles across his nose. And then, bringing up the rear was our little brother Mac. We had to stop calling him "little" - at just three years old, he looked more like four. He was tall for his age, and had a round belly. So that's about how we looked, I suppose, to Mrs. Wheeler as she moved in with her boxes and a heavy trunk and took over our household.

Ours was a small mixed farm: milk cows, and other cattle, pigs, chickens, and three horses. Dad had an old truck that required constant repair, and a small tractor. We had lots of cats, and each spring there were kittens for us to claim and cuddle. Our farm dog was Skipper, both a pet and a worker. He had his job to do, and he did it well. He kept the cattle in line, accompanied us when we went to the pasture to find the cows each afternoon, and he never failed to bark when someone came in the yard. Another role he played was to bolster our courage when we had to do something alone, such as go to the outhouse in the dark. We had no fear when Skipper was with us.

Our house was far from fancy. Even though we got "the power" when I was seven, we had only a few electrical appliances. Now that we could snap on the light switch, I sometimes thought back to those days with the coal oil lamp on the middle of the table, casting shadows on the walls in the evening. At the end of the day, Dad blew out the lamp and found his way upstairs to join Mom. There were two bedrooms upstairs: Mom and Dad's, with pink, flowered wallpaper, and the other one with two beds in it, where my four brothers slept. My corner was a partially closed-in space in the living room under the stairs. I slept there on a cot. I often had to order the boys out of my area, as when they played there, they always messed it up.

We still used an old-fashioned cookstove, which was always hungry for wood and kindling. We kept the reservoir on the side of it filled, so water was handy, and often warm enough to use for washing dishes.

After Mom died, we had to change things around for sleeping arrangements. Dad slept downstairs, which was convenient for him to tend to the stove. I, being the only girl, had no choice but to move upstairs, and sleep in Mom and Dad's room with Aunt Hazel for a couple of weeks, then with old Aunt Min, and in the summer with Mrs. Wheeler. She was a hefty lady, a grandmother type, and she wore a long flannel nightgown to bed. Our room was unbearably hot some nights, and we didn't even need to cover up with a sheet. She probably wished for a room of her own as much as I did, but it was all we had.

Looking back, I realize our family was a real handful, and probably the work was too hard for her. Some days when she was in a bad mood, she gave us dirty looks, and we were left to question what we had done to displease her. She was happiest when she was baking, and so were we! She could whip up a cake in jig time, and she made pies every Saturday. Will suggested we tell her how delicious the food was, so she would keep it coming.

Mrs. Wheeler stayed till the end of August. Of course, we worked alongside her, picking beans and shelling peas for her to can, and we pitched in to help preserve the other garden produce. Potatoes, carrots, turnips, and onions would be harvested later and stored in the cellar, so Mrs. Wheeler missed out on that.

By the end of the month, she'd had enough of us kids and the work. She collected her wages, and boarded the train to a town down the line where her son lived. She said he needed her help in his store.

BACK TO SCHOOL

September 1955

At the end of the end of August the school bell rang, calling us back to Briar Rose #221, our one-room school. Those were the hardest days for us kids. It took us back to before the summer holidays, to June, when we lost our mom. It was strange now, coming home to an empty house. Mom had always been there when we arrived, greeting us with a smile and some sort of snack: cookies, sometimes bread and jam. She was the heart and soul of our family, and now we were alone. None of us admitted it, but we even missed Mrs. Wheeler. Having someone in the house after school would have helped. The house was empty, and so were we.

We were on our own. Now that school had started again, and the housekeeper was long gone, Dad dropped off Mac with Mrs. Fiske each morning. He liked going there, and she called him her "little man". Dad picked him up in the afternoons, about the time we got home from school.

Roy, Will, Nick, and I usually enjoyed the buggy ride from school. It was freeing to be out of the stuffy classroom, and clipping along towards home in the afternoon breeze. Queenie was in a hurry on the home stretch, so it was faster than our leisurely morning ride. As they say, a horse can "smell the barn". Sometimes, my brothers and I talked on the way about what we had done at recess, or about Miss Locken's new ideas for the upcoming year. But as we turned in the lane, our conversation went silent. I remembered the exact spot where the cop car had been parked. Our mood soured as we neared the house, and the minute we walked inside, we were down in the dumps. Every day, I thought of the other kids from our school being welcomed home by their waiting mothers.

It was Roy's idea for us to play awhile before we had to start our chores. We hurried through a piece of bread, and then we ran out to the yard. Roy marked off a playing area west of the house with a couple of sticks at either end for goals. Will stuffed an old sugar sack tight with rags and grass, and tied it shut with binder twine. That was our soccer ball.

Our teams were always the same. The fairest arrangement was Roy, the oldest, with Nick the youngest. Will and I, the middlers, formed the opposing team, and did we have fun! We ran full tilt, till our faces were red trying to get to the ball first. If we got our hands on it, we threw it with all our might between the goal sticks. Sometimes a strong kick pushed it through.

Roy was careful to keep track of the time. If Dad was already in the yard, of course we didn't play at all. Or even if our game was beginning, and we heard his truck coming from picking up Mac from Fiske's, we hid the ball and quickly went to our work. On the days when the coast was clear, we played for half an hour, while Roy kept score. Our teams were evenly matched, so sometimes Will and I won, sometimes Roy and Nick. For a couple of weeks, we played every day that we could when we got home. The next Monday, our game was well underway when Nick lied. He said the ball had gone between our goal sticks and we all knew it hadn't. I was already in a bad mood, and I was hot and mad.

"I don't play with liars," I yelled and stomped off the field. I wanted to be away from them. It wasn't about the game. Nick could be a little liar if he wanted to. *I* didn't care! As I marched toward the house, I knew very well what it was. I was plain and simple lonesome for my mom. How could we go *on* this way without her? Nick caught up with me and pulled on my hand.

"Dottie, don't go in. I'm sorry." Nick was crying.

"What's the matter with you?" I tried to shake his hand off my arm. "It's a stupid game, with a stupid ball, stuffed with rags."

We stopped on the doorstep. I didn't want to open the door, and go into that empty kitchen again. It bothered me that tears were falling down his face. He looked extra small, and he was barefoot. He always kicked off his shoes as soon as we got home. I knew I was being harsh, probably to keep from crying myself. "Why do you care if we play or not?"

He answered quickly, even though he was still sniffling. "'Cause if we don't play our game after school, there's nothing to look forward to in the whole day."

I had a strange and sudden feeling. I felt tall, so tall I could look down on our yard. I could see four young kids, desperately getting by, alone and lonely. I let Nick keep holding my hand. I yelled back to Roy and Will, "Okay, let's play!"

In the days after, I kept seeing Nick as he was - not yet six years old, little and sad - and I started being nicer to him. I helped him get washed up before we left for school, and played guessing games with him as we both sat in the tight space at the back of the buggy.

One of my Friday spelling words was *pathetic*. When I wrote down the meaning of it, I thought, "That's us. That's us Cleaver kids. Our life is pathetic." The boys were as lost and lonely as I was.

NICK GETS SICK

It was a few days later that Nick got sick. It was Saturday afternoon, and I couldn't find him. I was planning to get after him because it was late, and he hadn't started to fill the wood box. I needed wood to get a fire going, so Will and I could cook something for supper. I finally hunted him down, and there he was in the upstairs bedroom, all curled up under the blankets. I yanked back the top quilt, and yelled, "What the heck, Nick? You can't get out of your chores that easy!"

My words faded away when I saw his closed eyes, and his red cheeks. I was going to say a lot more. Like that I'd been working in the kitchen by myself, and he'd better not expect me to help with the wood. Instead, I touched his forehead.

"Nick, you're hot!"

"I know." His voice was a whisper. He closed his eyes again like he had a headache, and croaked out, "My throat is so sore, I can't swallow."

I put a pillow behind his back, and sat him up a bit. I turned his head towards the window, and told him to open up. Seeing how red this throat was, I ran down the stairs, and got a cup of water out of the water pail. When I came back into the room, he had slumped down, but I got the pillow stuffed behind him again. I saw how carefully he swallowed a couple of sips. He wasn't pretending. He huddled under the covers again. I felt guilty. He looked so small, the same as the day I said I didn't want to play with the rag ball.

"Don't worry about the wood, Nick. Can you try to drink a bit more?"

He didn't answer. I was trying to figure out what to do. "When it's ready, I'll bring some supper up here for you."

His eyes opened wide. "No don't. I can't eat! Honest, I can't!"

I got Mac and Will to start filling the wood box and tried to think of what I should make for supper. I tried to remember the last time one of us was sick. We had all had colds in the winter, and we rubbed up with Vicks, and stayed home from school for a day or two. Roy stepped on a nail last summer and had to get a shot. Other than that, I guess we were a healthy bunch. I couldn't remember ever being very sick myself, for sure nothing like the sore throat Nick had today. I took more water up to him, and forced him to drink a little. I put a wet cloth on his head, but he pushed it away, and said it gave him the shivers.

Dad came in at suppertime and sat at the table. All I'd made was sandwiches, because I couldn't get the fire going, and I was too worried about Nick to think of making anything better. Dad was quiet as ever, and we were quiet, too, as we ate. I waited for Dad to ask where Nick was, but he didn't. I was getting madder at him as the minutes passed. Didn't he care? Wouldn't a dad notice one of his kids wasn't at the table? When he pushed back his chair like every other evening, I knew he would go sit by the stove and light a cigarette.

I said, quite loud, "Nick's sick!" I said it louder than I planned to. Dad turned towards me and narrowed his eyes. "Is the wood box full?"

Something exploded in my head at that second. I never talked back to Dad, at least not out loud. Only in my mind. I was wishing we had a dad who made a decent life for us, a dad like the neighbor kids had. I was thinking of that day when Nick said, "If we don't play after school, there's nothing good in the whole day."

I guess in a way, I felt I was sticking up for Nick when I yelled out, "So that's all you care about - about how much work we get done!" I could hardly believe I said it, and I knew I was louder even than when I first blurted out that Nick was sick.

I kept at it. This time I was yelling. "He's *sick*, Dad, he's *really* sick!" I could see Roy and Will were as shocked at my outburst as Dad was.

Dad ignored me, as he reached for his yellow Vogue tobacco can above the stove. He was intent on rolling his smoke, while I took

17

water upstairs for Nick. I didn't know what else to do, so I kept trying to make him drink water. What would Mom do? This time, I could tell Nick was even hotter than before and he didn't move at all when I touched his forehead.

"Nick... Nicky?" I hadn't called him that for a long time. His lips were bright red. I went downstairs for a spoon, and had to walk past Dad on my way to the cupboard. The air around him was blue with smoke. What kind of a parent doesn't check on a sick kid? The boys had disappeared, and the table was as we left it. I stared at Dad as I passed his chair, and he stared back, as if we were kids having a staring match.

Back in his room, I spooned some water into Nick as he lay there. It dribbled off his face, and onto the pillow. Downstairs again, I decided to clean up the kitchen. I took the dishpan outside to get water from the rain barrel under the eavestrough at the corner of the house. When I was out there, I thought I heard Nick moan or call out something. Up I went again, but he wasn't moving. Will was waiting for me at the bottom of the stairs.

"Is he going to die?" he asked. I stared at him for a second, and then looked over at Dad.

"He might. People die in this house and nobody cares!"

I don't think I'll ever forget the look on Dad's face. Of course, I don't know what he was thinking, but I know he had murder in his eyes. He must have known I was accusing him about Mom.

My thoughts were going a mile a minute. Serves him right for never talking to us about her. I didn't know what was going to happen. I could feel the air crackling. As I cleared the plates off the table, Dad went out, slammed the door behind him - not a word. To me, his silence was always worse than if he swore at us. I continued washing the dishes by myself, no help from Nick tonight.

Roy turned on the radio. That was a bold move! Dad was the one in charge of that.

"Where do you think he went?" I asked Roy.

Roy answered with a shrug, "I guess for the doctor after what you said."

I told Roy I hoped he had, but I doubted he would, since he never even went and checked on Nick.

"Oh yes, he *did*," Roy said, sitting closer to the radio. "He went up there, when you went outside with the dishpan. So did I."

"Did he say anything?"

"Yeah. I heard him say, 'It's bad.' Then he came down and put on his boots. You know the rest."

Yes, I did know the rest. I realized now that he was already going for the doctor, when I slammed him about Mom. Of course, I shouldn't have said what I did about people dying in this house, but I wasn`t sorry. Not one bit. I had decided a while back that I would wait it out till I was sixteen. If he didn't come clean about what happened to Mom, then I'd find a place. I'd find somewhere else to live. Every time I looked at him, I thought, "My dad is a murderer!"

GOOD THINGS
COME FROM BAD

When bad things happen, like Nick getting sick, we think it is the worst, but sometimes it turns out for the best. That's how it went for us that fall. The doctor made Dad hire a trained nurse, and she stayed with us for a week, and what a glorious week that was! Her name was Mrs. Carson, and she was patient and kind to us all, not only to Nick. She must have figured since we were all kids, she would be the one to cook for us, so I was off the hook. She told Dad what groceries to buy, and he did so, quite agreeably. We had the best school lunches that we'd ever had, even bananas, and cheese sandwiches. And she made them for us, too, instead of us trying to do it as we rushed out to the buggy. I did Nick's wood chores for the whole week, but that was nothing, compared to trying to cook something for supper, and cleaning the kitchen. I'm sure Nick felt like a young prince as he rested downstairs on the couch with pillows and a blanket, under the nurse's watchful eye.

I helped her with the dishes, and the boys did their regular chores. Roy didn't go to school at all that week, because it was harvest time, and he was needed to drive the tractor, while Dad rode the binder. It was so fascinating to see how the binder wound a piece of twine neatly around each sheaf, and even tied a knot, before kicking it out onto the field.

We had a nurse in the house, and she gave us strict lessons about washing our hands before we ate, and after we went to the outhouse. Mrs. Carson often put clean water in the basin for us, and made sure we knew how to use the bar of red Lifebuoy soap on our face and hands. She was especially kind to Mac, and he followed her all day long. Since she was a nurse, I asked if she knew why Nick got sick. She said he had strep throat, and the germs could spread very easily to each person in a family, especially when we drank out of the same dipper. We sure didn't have enough clean cups for each person to have a different one every time we wanted a drink. So, we kept using the dipper, but we took a small amount, so we could throw our dregs away, and not back into the water pail.

My brothers were as sad as I was to see her pack up her smooth, brown suitcase on Saturday afternoon, exactly one week after Nick took sick. We'd had a glimpse of what life could be like, what it should be like, for a family of farm kids on the prairie. I remember thinking that if I ever got kids, I would be nice to them like Mrs. Carson was to us, and I wouldn't expect them to work like adults.

Maybe it was Nick getting sick like that, so bad and so suddenly, that made Dad realize he needed to try for a housekeeper again. He must have known someone had to run the house and kids while he did the farm work. Or, maybe he had some extra money, because everyone was saying this harvest was a bumper crop, which might mean he could afford to hire a housekeeper for the winter.

THE BULLY

T he school year had started near the end of August, and the best part on the first day was to see Miss Locken again. No doubt she went shopping during the holidays, as she wore a different pretty dress each day, and white Mary Jane shoes with a black strap at the front. She often wore clip-on earrings to match the color of her dress. I noticed her blond hair was cut shorter than before, and she must have taken the time to set it each night with pin-curls. All of the girls dreamed of looking like her when we grew up, but mostly, I wished to turn out as kind and thoughtful as she was. She took time for each student and she often said, "Don't be scared to share a smile. It won't cost you a cent!"

I wondered what she would do if the school bully got nasty again. I had a feeling she was ready for it. Last year, she wasted no time calling Bud Turner, the head of the school board, when she needed him. He came into the school and straightened things out.

That was a day to remember! It was all because of a very small issue - doing school chores. Each week, Miss Locken assigned various tasks to students, like cleaning the blackboards, taking the brushes outside and banging the chalk out of them, emptying the wastebasket, putting up and taking down the flag morning and afternoon - easy jobs like that. She said it was to teach us to take pride in our school, and to work as a team. So, it happened that one Monday when Miss Locken wrote the list on the board, Bob Walker was tagged to clean the brushes for the week. His name was Bob, but known to us younger kids as Bully Bob, or BB for short. Of course, we never let him catch us calling him that, because we were scared of him. He was mean, even mean to his horse, who stood out in the barn with the other horses all day waiting for 3:30, when school was out. He was taller than Miss Locken, and had a bad attitude. As the school day ended, the teacher reminded the ones who were on the chore list, and everyone began their duties. Everyone except BB. As he hadn't moved from his desk, Miss Locken said, "Bob, its time."

He was ready with a smart answer. He looked straight at her. "Yep, its time all right. Time you started doing your work around here, since you're the one getting paid."

Miss Locken opened her mouth, then closed it. She quickly walked to the back of the room, where the phone hung on the wall. She lifted the receiver from the left side of the wooden phone box, and held it to her ear. With her right hand, she grabbed the handle, and cranked out one long and three shorts. The twin silver bells at the top of the phone made a muffled, ringing sound. She spoke up into the mouthpiece that stuck out almost above her head. Her side of the conversation went like this: "Hello, Mr. Turner. I'm glad you're home. We need your help at the school to deal with Bob Walker. Yes, I'll keep the students in until you come. Goodbye."

No one moved, except the ones who were doing the other chores. Fortunately, Bud Turner lived less than a mile from the school and he had a small, black car that he called The Coupe. In no time at all, Bud came striding through the open door, and stopped in front of BB's desk. Funny how small Bully Bob suddenly looked! Mr. Turner was tall and broad, with a bushy, black mustache. He leaned forward, and placed both hands flat on BB's desk. In a booming voice he asked, "What's going on, Bob?"

Bob stammered a little. "I...I'm not doing brushes. I don't like getting that yellow chalk dust on my hands."

"Really! A big guy like you scared of a little chalk dust! I think we'll help you get used to it. You can clean all the brushes every day till Christmas."

A gasp went up from different directions of the room. It was a relief for us all to see the bully knuckle under for a change. Bud Turner had more to say.

"Bob, look at me. This is it! You give the teacher, or the students, any trouble of any kind, and I'll kick you out of this school!"

You could have heard a pin drop. Mr. Turner nodded to Miss Locken, and we heard his little car start up, and zip out of the schoolyard. So that was last year. I had a feeling Bob would give it another try this year. I kind of wished he would, because it would be exciting to watch, but I knew I would feel sorry for Miss Locken. Even though the bully had grown a lot taller over the summer, I was sure Miss Locken would stand up to him if there was a showdown.

If she was worried about Bob, she hid her fears from us and talked about her brand-new ideas for the school year, like spelling bees, geography matches, and music on Friday afternoons. She told us there was still time to get our school entry in for Saskatchewan's Golden Jubilee competition. I didn't even know what a Golden Jubilee was, but she made it sound exciting. She convinced us we were in for a fantastic ride this year, even though we were only 16 students in total attending the Briar Rose School.

SIGNS OF AUTUMN

Our school day started when the bell rang at nine in the morning. First, we stood beside our desks and repeated the Lord's Prayer. Miss Locken had printed a poem on the blackboard, which we read in unison each morning to help us memorize it. It was a well-chosen poem called "September", and was all about summer being over, and autumn's arrival. She made sure we knew the name of the poet who wrote it, Helen Hunt Jackson. By the second time I read it, I had learned the first four lines by heart:

> The goldenrod is yellow,
> The corn is turning brown;
> The trees in apple orchards
> With fruit are bending down.

Of course, we didn't have any apple orchards in our area. There were a few scraggly old crab apple trees in some yards, but the apples were sour and small. I liked the sound of the "September" poem, the sing-song way the words went together, and I memorized it as quickly as the older students. I decided Grade 5 was going to be A-okay.

The fall mornings were fresh, but still warm. Nick and I squeezed into our familiar spot in the back of the buggy, and as we rolled along, we watched for signs of fall to report to Miss Locken. She wrote the students' observations on the blackboard, and added to the list as the days went by. The purple flowers of the fireweed grew on a tall stalk, and had been around all summer. Nick and I could see that the very last buds at the top end of each stalk were opening now, another sign of fall.

As we passed Garnet's slough near the school, we saw a few mallard ducks swimming around in the middle of the water. Nick and I decided to ask Miss Locken when the ducks would go south, and how far they would have to fly before they reached their wintering grounds. Nick caught sight of a male duck near the road. The morning sun was shining directly on its emerald green, feathered head. Nick had a special interest in birds, so I explained that it's the male duck, called a drake, who has a green head. Nick planned to tell Miss Locken the ducks were getting ready to fly south.

Nick was a quick learner, and he easily got the hang of reading. He fell in love with Dick and Jane, Sally and the dog, Spot. I remembered I felt the same in Grade 1. I couldn't get enough of the simple stories and pictures that made us laugh. "Oh Dick. Come here. Get Spot. Run, Dick, run!" Of course, in the one-room school, we heard the lessons for every grade. We all remembered the magic of learning to read, and smiled as our little brothers or sisters stumbled over the words, "Oh Dick, come here."

As for me, I was sailing into Grade 5 and my reader was *Wide Open Windows*. I read ahead when I had free time, because I loved the stories. I had heard them all before, when I was in the lower grades.

A handwashing station was set up at the back of the room. At noon, the teacher poured water in the basin and let the youngest kids wash their hands. Nick was proud, as Mrs. Carson had taught him all about the correct way to use that Lifebuoy bar of soap! Miss Locken replaced the dirty water with clean a few times, and when all 16 students had washed, we were dismissed for the noon hour. Water was never wasted. It was brought to school in a metal container to be used for our drinking water, and also for handwashing. There was a four-gallon crock with a tap that held our drinking water, and beside it were three cups upside down, on a paper towel.

Recess was the best time of all. Steal Sticks required two teams, as it was somewhat like our soccer game at home. Nick was as fast as lightning, and the older kids soon pegged him as the one to guard the sticks even though he was a Grade "one-er". The teacher often got us started choosing up sides for a ball game at the noon hour, and then she went off to her little house to have her lunch, and keep an eye on us through the window. We played other games too, like Pum-Pum-Pull-Away, which was a running game that got our blood pumping.

Of course, Lemonade in the Shade was a favorite, a basic game of charades. One team came marching towards the other, and the words went back and forth:

Team one shouted, *"Here we come!"*

The other team, *"Where from?"*

"Tennessee!" (We had no clue where Tennessee was.)

"What's your trade?"

"Many motions."

"Show us some!"

Team one then began to act out an activity, or maybe an animal. As soon as the other team guessed correctly, team one ran back to their line, with team two in hot pursuit. Whoever they caught, joined their team.

Nick loved the games, and something we hadn't noticed at home - he was quite the little joker. Even the oldest kids thought he was funny, and he loved making them laugh. Miss Locken was especially kind to him, and gave him a harder book to practice reading, because he already knew all the Dick and Jane words.

I didn't have a "best friend" at school, but I ran along with the girls, when they went to eat lunch outside in the maple trees, or sometimes in a grassy spot by the teacher's house. It was called a "teacherage", and was provided by the school district so the teacher did not have to board with one of the school families.

One girl - her name was Maxine - kept bragging about the electrical appliances in her home. They had a toaster and an iron. Big deal! The rest of us got tired of hearing it.

School was shaping up, but with Mrs. Carson gone, life took a downturn at home. I could tell we were losing ground, because we were so mean to each other. Will and Roy were always scrapping. Dad and Roy hardly ever spoke to each other. I could feel the tension between them, and I hated that. I was tired of trying to be the peacemaker, and I stared at Dad, at the back of his head, trying to figure out if he was a killer. If he was, how safe were we? Who was next? Then I'd tell myself my wild thoughts were racing away on me.

One night, when Dad and Roy were out at the barn and Will and I were doing dishes, I said, "Tell me the truth, Will. Do you think Dad killed Mom?"

He looked surprised. His eyebrows went up. "What? You're crazy! Of *course* he didn't!"

"So, do you have a better explanation?"

"Well, I think she maybe was going to have a baby."

"So? People don't die of that!"

"Yeah, they do sometimes. Dot, forget I said it. I don't know for sure."

"Here's my next question. Do you think Mac is okay?"

"Yeah, why?"

"He used to talk a lot, but not anymore. He's three years old, and he just points to things he wants. I'm worried about him."

"He'll be okay, Dot." There was a lot to think about.

We didn't play soccer after Nicky got sick. The weather was getting colder. Dad was still harvesting the crop, and needed the older boys' help more than ever. I often played "Farm" before bed with Nick and Mac to keep them happy. We had quite a few toy farm animals, and the boys always wanted me to join their game. That way, they didn't fight so much.

WHO IS LIZ?

We came home from school two weeks after Mrs. Carson left, and as the buggy bounced in the lane, I caught sight of a woman standing on the step. She had her arms crossed over her chest as she watched us approach. When we got closer, the main thing I saw about her was her extra-large eyes, as they were sort of bugged out, and she had a huge smile. Now what? Why would this stranger be standing in our door waving to us?

She wasted no time introducing herself. As soon as we were close enough to hear, she said loudly, "Hello. I'm Liz. I'm Liz Parker."

We eyed her suspiciously, and Nick asked, "Does Dad know you're here?"

"Well, of course he does! He gave me a ride here this morning." We couldn't help but stare at her.

"As awful as it sounds, I'm the new housekeeper!" She said the word "housekeeper" in a creepy voice, and wiggled her fingers in the air. Her extra-wide smile made it even scarier.

She motioned to Roy and Will to come over to where we were standing. Will came, but Roy looked the other way and took Queenie to the water trough. We all knew he wasn't exactly the friendly type - never had been. I was trying to get my mind past this woman's huge eyes, and I guess I did, because suddenly it felt comforting to have someone waiting on the step watching for us to come home from school.

About that time, Mac came running outside, and pointed to Liz like she was really big news, which she was! I could smell something baking in the oven. Maybe cookies? My heart was jumping inside. I wanted this to be true, not some crazy dream. For so long now, I longed for someone to look after us, to take care of Mac, and to help

Nicky get ready for school in the mornings, to make our lunches. I knew I was already putting too much hope into what probably wouldn't pan out.

Liz looked at me intently, almost too intently, and smiled that wide, toothy smile. "So, you're the girl! Your dad says you know how to work."

Then she looked at Nick and Will, who had parked at the table, in hopes of the treat that was soon to come out of the oven.

"Mac and I made cookies. I hope they pass your inspection!"

Why was this woman taking over the kitchen? I wished Dad would talk to us when he made plans, especially something like a new housekeeper! We knew for two days before old Aunt Min came, just long enough to get excited about her dog, and as it turned out, we shouldn't have bothered. When he hired Mrs. Wheeler, we never knew until she was already here, and bossing us into fetching water and wood. Now today, we come home on an ordinary day from school, feeling sad that Mrs. Carson the nurse, was gone, and here's this tall new woman running our house.

She turned to me with her large, brown eyes and said, "I hope raisin cookies are okay."

I nodded, admitting, "We like almost everything!"

The cookies were golden brown, and as she slid them, piping hot, onto a dinner plate, I could tell she knew her way around a kitchen! I wondered who she was and where she came from. Here she was, making herself so much at home in our house that we suddenly felt like it was her place, and not ours.

"Two each!" she said, with another grin.

Roy came through the door, and Liz was there, holding out her hand.

"I'm Liz."

Roy shook hands, and said "Roy." He sounded like a grown-up. He grabbed a couple of cookies, and took a bite of one. He grinned, "Not bad." Wow, we didn't usually see Roy this friendly. They say the way to a man's heart is through his stomach. Roy was 14, but maybe he was growing into a man, and he liked the way she showed him respect by shaking his hand. I guess he liked the cookies, too.

Mac was already comfortable with Liz, pulling on her blue apron, and pointing for another cookie. She held one out to him and said, "Say please..."

"Pease."

"That's a good boy. I like boys to be polite."

Nick took the hint. "Thanks for the cookies." He was such a fetching little boy, almost six years old, and taking in every detail of the world around him. As soccer was a thing of the past, Roy announced it was chore time.

Liz grinned, with that unnerving, oversize smile. "Wow, first polite, and hard workers to boot. I think I've just walked into heaven."

For a minute there was an awkward silence, and we stood still, kind of dazed. Liz gave Nick a playful push, "Don't let me hold you up! Go for your chores."

Roy and Will headed towards the barn, Nick and I to the wood-pile. We saw Mac grab Liz by her apron string, and point to the water pail.

"Use your words, Mac."

"Wader."

"Good boy." Liz poured a drink from the dipper into a cup, and handed it to Mac.

"Pease."

We had been trying to make him talk for months. It seemed Liz had cast a spell on him. Nick and I filled the wood box in record time. I wanted to see what she was up to next, and I wondered about supper. She had a hot fire burning in the cookstove, and the tea kettle was boiling.

This woman had come in like a tornado, and had taken over the Cleaver household. I remember thinking, life will never be the same again. Maybe we had just walked into heaven, too.

I'LL TELL YOU WHAT

I would have to say Liz came in the nick of time. I don't know where Dad found her. There were ads in the back section of the *Winnipeg Free Press* and *The Family Herald*. Maybe he placed an ad, and Liz responded to it. I could imagine Dad wording his request. "WANTED: Housekeeper for a family of five children ages three to 14, located on a farm near McKeen, Saskatchewan." Or, maybe Aunt Hazel knew about her and told Dad, or perhaps the idea came from Mrs. Fiske.

I couldn't help but like Liz. My brothers did too, but Dad didn't seem to think much of her. Liz was fun, and she told stories that were so weird we couldn't possibly believe them, yet we begged for more.

Life was better than it had been since the awful day in June when we lost our mom. I knew Liz could never be a substitute for Mom. No one could ever take her place.

The memories I had of Mom were fading a bit, and I felt sad about that. I had two that I often thought of, before I fell asleep at night. One was the time she and I found a clump of violets in the bush on the edge of the yard. We carefully dug them up, planted them beside the house, and watered them, every time they looked wilted. Mom's name was Violet, and probably that's why I chose it as my favorite flower.

My second special memory of being with Mom was watching a sunset together. As we were walking by the barn fence, after shutting the chickens in for the night, she glanced to the west, and said, "Dottie wait a minute. This is going to be a show!"

The sun was sinking, and sending up the most glorious orange rays, turning the clouds to varied shades of peach and purple. The edges of the clouds were tipped with gold, and it was breathtaking to see it changing, getting brighter and more beautiful by the second. We were leaning on the corral fence taking it all in. She put her hand on my shoulder. "I wonder, Dottie, if we're looking right into the gates of heaven?" Maybe when she left us, Mom found the answer to her question. All I know, is that I think of her every time I see a sunset.

Liz made us laugh. We never knew what she was going to say or do next. She often said, "I'll tell you what, Dot" - and then she would tell me something she wanted me to remember. One was to never take more than two cookies, even if someone offers you more. "You say, 'No thanks. They were delicious, but I've already had two.' That shows you're a polite kid, and not a glutton." I remember some of her other "I'll-tell-you-what-Dot" lessons. "If you make a cake, and it sinks in the middle and looks terrible, know what you do? You whip up the sweetest, fluffiest icing, and spread it all over that flopped cake. Fill the hole with icing and no one will know. All they'll know is that they love your cooking!"

"I'll tell you what Dot, if supper's not ready and the men are coming in to eat, fry a pan of onions. When they walk in they'll think a tasty meal is nearly ready, and worth waiting for!"

When she was on a roll like this, I tried to remember the different things she was teaching me. Then she'd say just as seriously, something like, "I'll tell you what, Dot - if you see a mouse in the house, grab it quick by the tail, and cook it up for breakfast!" And then she would break out in her great belly laugh. She loved her own jokes. We always snickered when she acted silly, because we couldn't help it. Even though we giggled out loud, Dad never laughed. He acted like he didn't even hear her.

Liz liked to kid around with Roy and Will. One time Roy was wondering if it was getting close to suppertime. He stuck his head in the kitchen doorway, and asked, "What time is it?"

Liz called back, "Half-past kissin' time, time to kiss again!" She was so busy cackling at her smart reply, that she didn't even check the clock to answer him correctly. Roy shook his head, and with that crooked grin of his, turned away from the screen door.

Liz took an interest in our school work. She made sure Nick and I brought home a list of our spelling words that were tested every Friday. She set us up with papers and pencils at the table and pretended to be a very strict teacher.

"Dorothy, sit up straight. Write the word 'courage'." Then she would make up a whacky sentence. "The boy had courage when he rode a pig."

Then it was Nicky's turn. "Nickolas, the word is 'jump'. Here's the sentence: Your dad will jump on the roof of the barn." Nick would go into peals of laughter, while Dad kept staring straight ahead, and listening to the radio. His expression never changed. And on it would go. So, it was no wonder we got our spelling words correct every Friday.

When we came home from school, Liz was always listening to *Let's Go West* on the radio, featuring the latest hit songs. She was usually humming along as she did her work. One song caught my interest, "In the Blue Canadian Rockies". It reminded me of Miss Locken's talk of the Rocky Mountains she had seen in the summer holidays. When I heard the song, I made myself a promise that I would see them, if it was the last thing I ever did.

I told Liz about my dream to travel to the Canadian Rockies. The next day, she handed me a notebook, with the words to the song written out in her loopy handwriting. She leaned over my shoulder, and sang the beginning few lines. I imagined the towering blue mountains, the waterfalls, and Lake Louise. Miss Locken said the lake, in Banff National Park, was named after Princess Louise, daughter of Queen Victoria. Our teacher never missed an opportunity to share new information.

At school, I had been working on a map of Canadian provinces, and I found out the mountains were in Alberta and British Columbia. Miss Locken spoke again of entering the Saskatchewan Golden Jubilee competition, and suggested I enter my map. She let us work on our various projects one whole Friday afternoon, instead of doing our usual school work.

As we worked, I asked Maxine, "What's the Golden Jubilee, anyway?"

Maxine looked at me like I was a dumbbell. "You don't know? It's Saskatchewan's 50th birthday this year! Fifty years since it became a province."

"And how am I supposed to know that?"

"Everybody knows it! We all went to the parade on Main Street in McKeen on July 1st. Don't you remember the floats and the costumes?"

Some of the other girls joined in, recalling the fun and the races and the free ice cream. I kept my head down, working on the outline of Saskatchewan. Our family didn't go to any Golden Jubilee. It was a hard summer without Mom, and we stayed home every day.

When I got home that night, I asked Liz if she knew about the Golden Jubilee. She said she did, and she listened while I told her about Maxine and the others telling me what I'd missed, and how Maxine made me feel dumb.

All Liz said was, "I'll tell you what, Dot - if someone is going to be mean, make sure it's not you!"

Then she grabbed a pan, and started heating it on the stove, with a little lard in it. She put in some popcorn seeds, and slid the pan back and forth over the surface of the hot stove. Soon we heard the pop-pop-popping as she held onto the handle with one hand, and the lid, covered with a potholder, with the other. When the "pops" let up a little, Liz dumped the hot popcorn into a large bowl, and added melted butter and salt. Now *that* was a treat! We didn't know she had popcorn on hand. We'd never had it at home before. I knew she had gone to town with Dad that morning for groceries, because she gave us each a stick of gum when we came through the door after school. The popcorn disappeared so fast, she made three batches. Dad and Roy liked it as much as the rest of us. After I went to bed, I thought to myself, "Liz pulled out the popcorn because she felt bad Maxine had been mean to me."

Another treat was puffed wheat cake. Liz told me it was the easiest recipe to remember, as it was also known as "Half-cup Cake". It called for a half cup of white sugar, half cup of butter and half cup of corn syrup. Add some cocoa, cook till bubbly and stir in puffed wheat. Mom used to make it, and we loved it. Liz served up a large piece to each of us after school. She was always talking.

"See, I told you I'd fatten up you Cleaver kids!"

Nicky set his piece down on the oilcloth that covered the table, and said slightly above a whisper, "Mom's is better." Liz was washing the puffed wheat pan and the wooden spoon. She quickly dried off her hands on her apron, and edged her way onto the bench where Nicky was sitting. She put her arm around him, and said, "I bet she made the best of everything! I'm so sorry I didn't get to meet her." Nick's tears were falling. "I know a little bit of how you feel, Nicky. I didn't have a mom when I was in Grade 1 either."

That was the closest Liz came to telling us about her life. It gave Nicky comfort. He finished his cake and asked for another piece.

"Here you go, Nick. But remember, only two!"

That night, before we fell asleep, I asked Liz if it was true about her not having a Mom when she was little, or did she make it up so Nick would feel better. She frowned at me and said, "Shame on you, Dot! You think I'd lie? Of course, it's true, I had no mama. That's what caught my eye when I saw your dad's ad in the paper."

So, he *had* placed an ad.

"The ad said 'Wanted a housekeeper for five children, ages three to 14.' All I could think of when I read it was, 'I'm going to get that job, and see if I can make those kids laugh again.'"

I got up my courage to ask another question. It was easier to ask in the dark.

"Liz."

"Mm-hmm?"

"Do you know how my mom died?"

"Nope, Honey-girl, I don't know. I never heard a word. I *do* know from watching that you are like a little mom to Nick and Mac."

I didn't say anything. I was thinking of the times when I hadn't been very kind to them. Liz thought I was nicer than I was. In a few seconds, it seemed, I could hear Liz snoring up a storm. Even old Aunt Min hadn't snored that loud!

JUST AROUND HOME

I am not sure what all a housekeeper is supposed to do, but I think the best explanation is she is paid to fill in for the woman of the house. Liz did everything. She must have been tired day in, day out. She kept us fed and our clothes clean. She washed the separator and the milk pails, washed the floors and dishes. She churned butter once a week in the dasher churn, sitting there for sometimes a half-hour, her arm going up and down with the plunger till the cream turned into butter. There were special meals to prepare when the neighbor men came for the sawing bee, or when someone came over to help butcher a pig or a steer. Such was life on the farm. I would guess a housekeeper in the city had a much easier time of it. Liz never told me where she had lived before, but I knew from watching her that she had worked hard in her life, and she knew all about the farm. Her hands were the hands of a working woman. She never complained about the work. She did more than the prescribed duties of a housekeeper, and for free, she threw in her bits of wisdom, and taught us her views of what is fair and proper.

Liz organized our Saturday baths much the same as my mom had done. She placed a boiler of water on the stove, late Saturday afternoon. It was the same process as heating water Monday mornings for washing clothes, except this time it was to wash *us*. The galvanized tub that leaned against the house by the rain barrel was brought inside, and tucked behind the stove. Liz rigged up a sheet to give privacy, and the baths began after supper, starting with Mac. Liz bribed him with a treat if he promised not to pee in the tub. We each took our turn with the bar of soap, including on our hair, and Liz added a little more hot water for each person.

One Saturday afternoon, Liz introduced a new recipe with the strangest name—Rickety Uncles. After we made and tested a batch, I knew it was going to be a favorite from now on. Liz wrote the recipe in my Blue Canadian Rockies notebook. It took a couple minutes to make --1/2 cup butter, ¾ cup brown sugar. Melt and add 2 cups rolled oats, 1 tsp vanilla, bake in the oven.

Dad had a barber set, which included a skinny, black comb, sharp scissors, and clippers. The box was kept at the top of the cupboard in the kitchen, and was used every couple of months when the kids' hair was getting shaggy. Dad put a chair in the middle of the living room, and started with Mac. By the time he was done, my poor little brother looked like a skinned rabbit, and then it was Nick's turn. Will got a haircut, too, although not as short, and when Dad looked over at Roy, all he got was a slight shake of his head. Dad didn't push it, and I was relieved for that. Liz had set out the Rickety Uncles that had been made in the afternoon and the boys enjoyed their bedtime snack.

Liz asked me if I wanted her to give me a trim. I said sure, because I was tired of my hair half-covering my eyes all the time. I sat in the chair, and I had a scary moment wondering if she had ever cut anyone's hair before. What if I got the cut of a lifetime like my poor brothers had! Oh, but of course, Liz *had* cut hair before. How could I doubt her! It seemed she had done most things and she was talented at everything. When she finished the trim, she brushed my hair and stuck a barrette on each side. She led me to the mirror over the basin.

"Now look at this little beauty!" she said, as she pushed me in front of the mirror. I couldn't believe how nice I looked. I was hoping she would help me make my hair look like that for school on Monday.

The Eaton's and Simpson Sears' catalogs were always somewhere in the living room, and were well worked over. Sometime in September, Dad told Liz to make an order for what winter clothes we needed. She had already started knitting socks and mittens for all of us. She also went through the boxes of our winter jackets and boots, checking to see what we needed.

"I'll tell you what, Dot, nobody has to always have brand new, and you remember that - hand-me-downs are okay!" She decided since Mac was such a solid boy, he could wear Nick's winter boots and coat from last year. Will could wear Roy's.

"Don't worry, Dot, I know how to make even old things look nice." I thought maybe she was bragging, but once again, as she attended to our winter clothes, she proved that she was accomplished in yet another area of expertise.

The Singer sewing machine sat in the corner and had not been used since Mom left us. One day, when I came home from school, there was a white blouse on my bed. Liz had followed me upstairs, I guess to see what I'd think of it. She seldom waited for me to speak, as she always had lots to say.

"So, you want to know where that came from?" She grinned. (Boy, were her teeth big!) "Well, I was walking past the sewing machine today, and suddenly it spit out that white blouse. I checked it over and thought it might fit you. Why don't you try it on?"

The next morning, I wore a white blouse and barrettes in my hair. Funny thing, Adele and Maxine were nicer to me than they'd ever been before.

Liz filled out the Eaton's order form, and let me have a look at it. She gave it to my dad, and he left the envelope open, so he could add a money order from the post office in McKeen. There was something ordered for all of us - whatever we needed to keep us warm, including new footwear for Dad. Nothing for Liz. When I asked, she told me she had everything she needed.

Roy and Will went out to help Dad with the milking each night after supper. They had started milking cows when they were younger than I was now, but Liz said, "I'll keep you busy here in the house. The best thing is not to learn how." So, every night, I jumped up right after supper, and got the dishwater heating as I cleared the table. Liz believed in kids having chores, and she often reminded us of the day she arrived when we got busy without being told.

Nick and I did the dishes on school nights. Sometimes he washed, sometimes dried, but Liz made sure we did each step properly. If there was more to do than usual, like washing bread pans, she helped us out. She had a deck of worn playing cards, and while Nick and I were doing the dishes, she sat at the table with Mac on her knee, and spread out the cards for solitaire. We soon saw that she spent more time teaching him the numbers than playing the game herself. Once we caught on to how solitaire was played, we loved to stand on either side of her and watch, pointing out where she could play a card.

I often had a night time question or two for Liz. One night I asked, "So do you know how to milk cows?"

"Of course, I do, Dot, but don't tell anybody!"

WINTER ON ITS WAY

October 1955

The weather was cooling off a lot, and Miss Locken had erased the "Signs of Autumn" and the "September" poem from the blackboard. If it had still been up, Nick could have offered one last observation. He was fascinated by the Canadian geese flying over our farm in the V formation, always pointing south. They flew high, but when we stopped to listen, we could hear their honk-honking cries, as they encouraged the rest of the flock.

About the middle of October, Miss Locken gave each family an envelope to take home for their parents. I got Liz to open it quickly, because I was curious. Inside, was a piece of cloth about ten inches long, and the same wide. The handwritten note with it said: "Dear Parents, A quilt will be raffled off to raise money for Christmas gifts for the students and preschoolers in the district. You may embroider any design you wish, including your name on this quilt block. Please return your completed block by October 31st. If you are unable to participate, please send it back to the school as soon as possible. Thank you for helping to make this a beautiful community treasure for the lucky winner."

Before I could start in about how I didn't even know what embroider meant, Liz said, very loud and exuberantly, "I'll tell you what, Dot, we are going to make the prettiest quilt block in all of Saskatchewan!" I was sure she was bragging again, but I remembered the blouse she made, and my nice haircut. She and I sketched different designs, and finally she said, "Here's what I think would be the best of all. Let's stitch *The Cleaver Family* in the middle of the block, and we'll do some pretty flowers all around the edge." I was totally in the dark. I didn't know what "embroider" meant, and whatever it was, I would likely make a mess of it.

Liz pulled out all the long, skinny sewing machine drawers, and lo and behold, in one of them she discovered plenty of embroidery cotton in several different colors. Now, I was getting the picture. By the end of the week, Liz had embroidered *The Cleaver Family* in a bright red color. She taught me how to thread the needle, and form little flower petals with a French knot inside each one. I practiced on a scrap piece of cloth, till Liz declared I was accomplished enough to make a border of flowers all around the edge. It turned out better than I had hoped. Liz filled in between each flower with green stitches that looked like leaves. It was a thing of beauty, and I proudly handed it in to Miss Locken, for the quilting ladies who would put it all together.

Dad must have gone to town during the day and got the mail, because when we came home from school, there was the Eaton's parcel on the kitchen table. Liz had waited to open it until we were there. It was an enormous one, wrapped in brown paper and tied with twine. Most everything we had ordered was correct, but a couple of things had been substituted. The timing of the parcel's arrival was perfect, because the weather was getting colder, and we needed warmer clothes.

Another parcel arrived the same week. It was from the woolen mills in Ontario. Soon after she came, Liz went through some boxes of clothes we had outgrown, sweaters, and anything made of wool. Dad found some additional items up in the attic, and when she had enough, she shipped it off. I had forgotten all about it. When the parcel came, they had made three blankets for us. They were grey, with a colored stripe across the top of each. She put two of the blankets in the boys' room and folded one for Dad on the couch. As she was bundling up the brown paper and string, she noticed something else.

"Aw Dottie, look! A little doll blanket! I remember they do this sometimes if there's a little extra wool." It was a pink and white blanket about a foot square with a white bunny in the middle.

"Here. Use it for your doll."

"Liz, I'm too old for dolls. I don't even have one."

By this time, I was used to Liz's eyes and her teeth, and I recognized her wicked smile when she was about to tease me. "Well, put the little blanket away. Someday, you'll have a baby girl, and she'll have a doll." I told her I didn't want a baby, and she quickly said, "You better not get one either, not for at least 25 years!" We both laughed.

Once the snow came, Dad drove us to school in the cutter each morning, and picked us up in the afternoons. We loved the cutter in the summer, because it was like a closed-in little house. It was parked by the bush, and Will and I, when we were younger, played house in there for hours. It had a bench at the back, a little stove that we never lit, of course, and a window at the front. In winter, it was quite a different story. We hated it! It was on sleigh runners, and pulled by our two horses, Danny and Moe. Dad called them "the team". The cutter ride over snow-covered roads was bumpy and rough, and we were squashed close together on the hard bench. The little stove belted out too much heat, and so we roasted in there with our coats and boots on.

The sound of the sleigh runners grinding over the snow made my head ache. It was always a relief to turn into the schoolyard, and get out into the fresh and freezing air. Dad sometimes took us to school in the open sleigh when the weather was warmer. That was much better than riding in the detestable cutter. We liked to hunker down, out of the chilly wind, and cuddle in a pile of straw and blankets on the floor of the sleigh box. On warmer days, we often ran behind the sleigh, and yelled for the horses to stop when we fell too far behind.

At home, there was a blazing fire in the stove all the time, and at night, Dad kept the heater stoked with coal, so we didn't freeze. Dad was sleeping on the click-clack couch anyway, so he kept both stoves fired up throughout the cold nights.

One night, I was awakened by the loud crack of a rifle in the middle of the night. My heart was thumping in my chest as I sat straight up in bed. I panicked.

"Liz!" She reached over, and patted my arm.

"It's a bitterly cold night, Dot. The nails in the house are pulling out of the wood. Go back to sleep." White frost often covered the nail heads showing through on our walls and ceilings. The fierce cold of winter was to be respected. On the coldest days, when it was minus forty and colder, Dad refused to take us to school, because he said it was too hard on the horses, and too dangerous for kids.

Liz baked giant loaves of bread, and sometimes a loaf burned black on the edge when it pressed against the inside edge of the oven. She had a sharp bread knife, and trimmed off the burned crust as if it never happened. One night, Liz suggested I make Poor Man's Pudding for dessert. I asked her how to do it, and she told me she had already written it in my recipe book. She wanted me to make it without any help, just by following the recipe.

I asked her why it was called Poor Man's Pudding, and she said because it didn't need any eggs, it was probably considered cheap to make. It turned out so tasty, with raisins and caramel sauce, that we decided to change the name in the recipe book to Rich Man's Pudding, as it was fit for a king.

HOME AND SCHOOL

November 1955

Miss Locken offered us an opportunity that came to her in the school mail. It was from the "Children's Bible Mission", a program for students to memorize verses from the Bible. It started when you learned one verse, and received a little, red book called the Gospel of John. Next, if you learned 25 verses you earned the New Testament; 25 more verses, a storybook; 50 verses, a wall plaque, and so on. I was very quick at memorizing, so I joined up and won three prizes. The Bible verses I learned were hard to understand, but I learned them word for word, and recited them to Miss Locken, who then let the Bible Mission know to mail another prize to me. I was proud of my winnings, and after I got the red book of John, I read a little of it each night before I went to sleep.

Nick was proud of my prize and, of all things, he showed it to Dad the night I brought it home. Dad recognized it right away as a book of the Bible and said, "I send her to school, not to church." Nick looked a little crushed, and handed it back to me. For a minute I felt like throwing it away. I could see the flames through the little mica windows in the heater door, and it would be so easy to toss it in, give my Dad a long look, and march upstairs to bed. I hesitated though, because Miss Locken had explained that some special verses in the red book were about heaven. I'd been thinking a lot about Mom. "In my Father's house are many mansions. If it were not so, I would have told you. I go to prepare a place for you." When the other students were out for recess, Miss Locken said it meant Jesus went to heaven to build beautiful houses for us to live in when we die. I hoped Mom was living in a tall white house, with climbing red roses, and violets all along the path to the door - and room for all of us.

I thought the girls at school would think I was silly to learn verses from the Bible, but they liked my prizes, and even Maxine said I was skilled at memorizing. I don't know if she meant it, or if she just wanted to use the word *skilled* as it was one of our spelling words for Friday dictation. The United Church of Canada held Sunday School once a month on Sunday afternoons in our school. I went a few times and I enjoyed being there, especially hearing the song they sang at the beginning.

> Count your blessings, name them one by one
> Count your blessings, see what God has done!
> Count your blessings, name them one by one,
> And it will surprise you what the Lord has done.

It was a catchy tune, and when I was singing a little of it at home, Liz joined in. She knew all the words, and belted it out. It lifted my spirits, and I think it did the same for her.

About that time, I began to see a pattern in Liz's moods. Some days she seemed a little too happy, getting silly and talking way too much. She was extra fun then, doing a happy dance as she worked, and saying the funniest things to make us laugh.

Dad told the older boys, with some disgust, "Look at her, she's high as a kite!" I sensed Liz was on the edge when her eyes were brighter than usual and a devil-may-care look came on her face that spelled a hint of trouble between her and Dad. Sure enough, her high mood would take her over the top, and the next days would prove to bring her down.

It didn't happen often though, and there was only one day in November, when she stayed the whole day in her room. For supper, I heated some leftovers, and carried a plate of food up to her while the others ate. Dad didn't say anything, but I could tell he wasn't happy, and he was watching her.

My older brothers were starting to argue a lot, even to the extent of some pushing and shoving in the living room after supper. I was certain Dad would take Will's side, and Roy would get the worst of it. Liz ignored their fighting, but she was well aware of it, as we all were. Maybe the winter was getting to them, being in the house so much.

One evening, when the boys were nasty with each other, out of the blue Liz asked, "Roy, do you know how to play crib?" She had her solitaire cards handy, and a homemade cribbage board with toothpicks for markers. Roy took to the game right away. After a few rounds, Liz looked at Will, her big eyes bigger than ever. "So, math wizard, give it a go." She left the cards on the top of the cupboard so Mac wouldn't lose them, and the boys played after that, almost every night. It was better to hear "Fifteen two, and the rest won't do," rather than the dreadful things they had been saying to each other before.

Nick was wishing he could play cards, too. Liz always came up with something, even a joke or a riddle. "Hey, Nick, Adam and Eve and Pinch-me went down to the river to bathe. Adam and Eve got drowned and who do you think was saved?"

Nick yelled out, "Pinch me!"

And Liz reached over and gave him a pinch on his arm. Then she laughed like crazy; Liz always laughed at her jokes. She reached her hands towards Nick, and laid her two fingers of one hand across two of the other. It made a square with a hole in the middle. "Put your finger in the crow's nest..."

"Come on Nick, put your finger in the crow's nest!" He cautiously put his finger in the space offered.

> Put your finger in the crow's nest
> The crow's not at home
> He's out behind the back door
> Peckin' on a bone!

As she said the last part, Liz squeezed her fingers together tightly, so he was caught. She pressed her thumbnail into his finger, and kept saying, "peckin' on a bone, peckin' on a bone." Nick was giggling, and wailing, "Ouch, ouch, ouch!" No doubt, he could hardly wait to try that trick on his friends at school. Nick called Mac, who eagerly put his finger in the crow's nest. Some practice on little brother proved to Nick he was going to have fun at recess tomorrow!

I was the girl with all the questions, and few answers. I had something to ask my older brothers, and I determined to do so when I got the chance. It came on a Saturday afternoon. Dad was outside, and Liz was upstairs in her room, having a tough day. So, I said to both of them, "I think we're all forgetting Mom."

Will looked puzzled, and said, "I'm not forgetting her."

I looked at Roy. His uncut hair was getting long and curly. "Roy?"

"I remember her pretty well. What do you think you're forgetting, Dot?"

I looked down. I was not going to do the tears. "Well, I'm forgetting her smile, and how she looked at us. I wonder lots of things. I don't remember - did she ever joke with us like Liz does? Did she get mad?"

Will looked like he might cry. Roy leaned towards me. I felt closer to Roy now than a few weeks ago. He was being nicer to us all.

"I don't think you're forgetting her, Dot. I think you're learning to live without her."

I managed a whisper, "Tell me what you remember."

My sensitive brother Will was on the verge of tears. "She did smile a lot," he said, "but she wasn't loud and funny like Liz."

"And she was quiet and nice," Roy added.

"Did she yell at us?"

"Um… sometimes, you know, when she had to. It's a mom's job."

I looked around the room. Nick and Mac were playing farm. The house was a bit messy. "Do you think she can see us here right now?"

Both my brothers shook their heads. "She's far," Roy said, "Really far."

I thought of the Bible verses I had learned at school to win those prizes - "In my Father's house are many mansions." I liked the sound of those words about heaven. Is that where she was?

Roy reached for the switch on the radio. Before he turned up the volume, he said, "Don't worry Dot, you'll never forget her. None of us will."

I don't know why Mom was so much on my mind in November. I remembered her tin trunk in the closet, and I wondered if it was still there. I knew exactly what it looked like. It was blue with gold, metal edges. The sides had a few dents in them. One night when Dad was out doing chores, I asked Liz if she thought I could look for it. She said she was the sneakiest snoop in the whole world, and she would help. We found the trunk easily enough in the bedroom closet. Liz put it on the bed and closed the door. She said if we got caught, she would take the blame.

I was hoping to find something special in there, and as I opened the lid, I noticed Liz had slipped out the door and downstairs. I think it would be called a keepsake trunk. Inside, were our baby bracelets, some first haircut curls, and a wedding picture. Wow, could that be Dad? He sure didn't look the same now. He was smiling in the picture, and Mom was beautiful, with long, dark hair and a white dress. She had written on the back of the picture: "Robert and Violet Cleaver, Wedding Day, June 19, 1940."

The trunk was about half full. I planned to go searching in it again and again, as there was lots to see, lots to remind me of my mom. A calendar from two years ago caught my eye. Mom had written our full names on the date we were born. On January 29, Will's birthday, she had written "William Stuart Cleaver, 1943." Of course, I flipped to the last month, December, and sure enough, on December 13th, Mom had written "Dorothy Elva Cleaver, 1945" and then my initials "DEC" as a monogram, with a heart around it. I realized DEC was short for December. Did she call me Dorothy Elva to fit that little puzzle, as she had with Mac's name? I would never know.

When I went downstairs, Dad was already back in the house, sitting by the radio, smoking. He didn't often go upstairs now that Liz and I had taken over his room, so there was no issue about him seeing the trunk on the bed. As I came into the living room, Liz put her hand on my shoulder. "Oh, by the way, Dot, your dad says you can keep the trunk."

A PERFECT DECEMBER

December was the best it could be. Every day felt like we had won a million bucks. Dad took us to school each day in the cutter, but we didn't mind it so much anymore, as fun things were happening at school. Miss Locken was pulling out all the stops for a top-drawer Christmas program. She promised it would be way better than last year, because she had a new book of plays and recitations. She handed out our parts for the plays early in December, and told us to learn our lines as soon as possible, so we could start rehearsing. Her favorite reminder to us was that "practice makes perfect".

I was in my glory! Memorizing was a challenge that I loved, and I had my parts learned in a couple of days. The plays and skits that Miss Locken came up with were funny, and even Bully Bob and all the older kids took part. The littlest students did the pageant, which was the story of Mary and Joseph going to Bethlehem. Maxine brought a doll to wrap up for the Baby Jesus, and we all sang "Away in a Manger". That part of the program ended with Edith Turner, dressed in a white gauze angel costume, singing a solo, "Angels We Have Heard on High".

Miss Locken asked us to hunt up props and costumes from home and we helped her make red elf hats from crepe paper. As we practiced and polished our performances, everyone's favorite play was called *Hec Says It!* It was about a guy trying to get up the nerve to ask a girl to marry him. Of course, there were lots of interruptions, but at the end of the play, Hec finally says it! In the play, Roy was Hec, the main character, and he did the best acting job you can imagine. The girl he was proposing to was, in real life, Louise Bell, who was quite shy, but she had a crush on my brother. All of us stopped doing our school work when they rehearsed. I was in that play, too, as I was one of the naughty children who interfered with Hec's proposal.

I just knew the whole month of December was going to be special. Of course, Christmas was coming and the Christmas concert was shaping up to be the best thing ever. Another event coming up was my birthday, on the 13th. I was counting on Liz to mark the day as she had for Nick. The cake she made for Nick's birthday in October was one of those that had the misfortune to sink in the middle. Maybe the oven heat wasn't even - Liz didn't know the problem - but she put me through a little review. "What did I tell you to do when a cake flops?"

I remembered her saying, "I'll tell you what, Dot...", and so I spread the icing extra thick to cover up the hole. She was right. No one noticed, and they loved the cake.

THE BLIZZARD OF '55

There was one unknown December event on its way. Not one of us had a clue it was coming. When it came, it was unforgettable, something I will remember all my life. Monday morning, December 12, the day before my 11th birthday, we loaded into the cutter, each with our lunch-kit, and with thoughts of a fun day at school getting ready for the concert. Dad sat on an old chair with no back on it, holding the lines that came through a hole under the window. The stove was close to his feet, and he had a pile of nice, little sticks prepared to add to the fire. He didn't say anything for the whole ride. All he did was hold the reins and yell at the horses now and then. It was a doubly long trip for him, as of course when we got out, he had to make the trip back home to start cleaning out the barn.

It seemed like a normal day, but it wasn't. Not at all. At the schoolyard, teams of horses pulling cutters were arriving in time for nine o'clock, and students were unloading, and heading to the school door. As we drove up, Stan Bell (that would be Louise's Dad) opened our cutter door and leaned inside. "Maybe I'm crazy, but I'm taking my kids back home with me. I don't like the sky in the west."

Dad said, "I had the same idea when we left home. Don't hurt them to miss a day." And that was it. We turned out the gate and back on the road we had come on, and Stan Bell's team was right behind us. It was the best decision. By the time we got home, the wind had picked up, and snow was coming down. It fell slowly at first, and then suddenly, the fury of the storm struck with full force.

Liz told Nick to stay inside with Mac, and she pulled on her boots and heavy coat to accompany Will and me to the woodpile. We brought load after load up close to the house, and when she finally

52

said it was enough, we each brought a staggering armload inside and dumped it on the living room floor by the heater. It was freezing cold out there, and my forehead hurt like someone had tightened a band of iron around it. I could tell the temperature was dropping, because inside my thick, woolen mitts my fingers were numb. By the time we got into the house, we couldn't see the barn, not even the outline of it. The wind was so strong, it was whipping the snow across the top of the windows. We waited for Roy and Dad to come in from the barn.

Fortunately, while we were gone, Liz had filled the barrel and the reservoir of the stove, as well as the boiler on top of the stove. She had packed them all tight with snow to melt for washing clothes, as it was Monday, after all. It was good she had all that snow on hand, as we would need it to get by in the house during the storm. Wash day could wait.

Will and I were chilled to the bone from our trips to the wood-pile and back, and Liz must have been, too. She said we needed a hot drink, to heat us from the inside out. She stirred cream, cocoa and sugar together, till the mixture was smooth, and then added it to a large saucepan of hot water on the stove. It was so delicious that I decided the recipe had to go into my special notebook. Liz would say it was too easy to bother writing down, but I wanted to have these recipes when I was older. We were still sitting there thawing out, and sipping the hot cocoa when Dad, Roy, and Skipper finally made it to the house. Roy's face was red with cold. Liz took a close look at him and instantly took note of two white spots, one on each cheek.

"Roy, you've got frostbite on your face. I need to take care of that." She helped him pull off his boots and coat and sat him down by the table. When he took off his toque, his long curls were sticking out every which way. She poured a cup of cocoa for Dad and Roy, and then went to work. She dipped two washcloths in warm water. She said the water couldn't be hot or cold, but the frozen skin needed to warm slowly. She told Roy it might feel prickly, but she didn't think it was bad enough to blister. Roy held the cloths on his cheeks till all the white was gone.

Dad was more talkative than usual. He told Liz about Stan Bell, and then we asked him if he had seen a storm like this before. He said he had seen some bad ones, but not coming so fast and furiously as this one did. He and Roy had been out at the barn so long, because they were hauling feed for the cows in the barn. They packed the feed into an empty stall, so they could get at it as the storm progressed. The other cattle were huddled in the three-sided lean-to. Our three horses were in their stalls in the barn, and Roy and Dad made sure they had hay and some grain. The barn would stay warm with all the animal bodies in there, but it would be worse for the ones outside in the lean-to. Liz worried about the chickens, but Dad said they had given them plenty of feed in the self-feeders and locked the door. The whole chicken house was already covered with snow. That would hold in the heat maybe, and he thought they would huddle together.

So, as the storm howled and whistled around the corners of the house outside, we were snug inside, and hoped the animals were surviving where they were. Dad turned on the radio. The reception was poor. Probably the wind was playing havoc with the aerial pole at the corner of the house. From what we could hear of it, the announcer from our closest radio station in the city where Aunt Hazel lived, was sending out warnings. "If you are safe and warm, stay where you are. Do not go on the roads. This storm is vicious." Throughout the day, they announced the frigid temperatures, the amount of snow coming down in record time, and over and over, the same warning, "Stay where you are. Stay safe. There is zero visibility."

On in the afternoon, Liz took it on herself to make a useful day of it. She looked through her mending basket and the button jar. She said it was time everyone learned how to sew on buttons. Nick and I were willing, but the older boys shook their heads when she said, "This means you, too." Liz persisted. "Every man should know how to sew on his buttons."

Will turned to Dad. "So, do you know how?" Dad more or less snorted. "No, I don't, but she's right. It's a great idea for you!" Roy got out of it because he and Dad had decided to do the evening chores early, while it was still light. The cows needed to be milked, and the stock fed. Roy's cheeks were still red, and Liz warned him if they got too cold, he was to come back in. It would harm the skin on his cheeks if it froze again.

Dad didn't argue when Liz insisted they tie the lines from laundry day to the radio pole attached to the outside the house. He and Roy dressed to go out, and Liz handed them each a blizzard mask of sorts that she had stitched up in the last hour. She combined two toques and made holes for eyes. She also made sure they were bound up with scarves, and extra socks, and double mitts. They looked like stuffed clowns but knowing how cold it was, they were willing. To please Liz, they tied the laundry lines around their waists. But I bet they were thankful for that security as they braved the blinding blizzard, trying to reach the barn. Before they stepped out into the storm, Dad said to Liz, "Keep Skipper in here, we almost lost him out there." Liz watched them from the window, but they were swallowed up in the wind and the snow almost as soon as they finished tying the line to the aerial pole.

We found it easy to get the hang of sewing on buttons. Liz had lots of missing spots on our shirts and blouses that had been waiting in the mending basket for such a day. And such a day it was!

Liz was determined we would practice for the concert to be sure we knew all our parts perfectly on the night of the 21st. The concert was ten days away, and she said the Cleaver family was going to shine! She had written down Nick's main recitation, and she had long ago learned the words to the familiar Christmas songs. So, we practiced as the day wore on, singing and reciting. Will and I had our play parts in our school bags. I hoped Roy had *Hec Says It* at home, too, so he could brush up on his lines.

Liz kept looking at the window, but of course, there was nothing visible. As the radio announcer had said, visibility was zero. She worried about Roy and Dad, and Liz was not one to keep her concerns to herself. "It's past time they should be back in here. If Roy freezes his face again, we will have real trouble on our hands." Her worried talk panicked Will and Nick, and they kept crowding with Liz by the window, seeing nothing. Finally, there was a bump and a bang on the door, and Dad and Roy burst in, looking more like snowmen than themselves. Balls of snow had collected on their heads, scarves, mitts, and masks, and stuck there. Liz helped them peel off the layers. They were cold, and they were exhausted. They didn't say much, but Liz had hot tea ready with milk and honey to warm them up. They were done for the night. They milked the cows, and gave it all to the pigs. If they had tried to carry it to the house, the merciless wind would have licked every drop out of the pails. Roy and Dad could hardly stay upright themselves, as they clung to the line that brought them back to the door. They reported all the animals were okay, except they hadn't got to the chicken house. The drifts were too deep. Liz worried about the hens, but didn't say anything. She realized Dad and Roy had done their best.

Roy put his head on the table and snoozed while Liz bustled around getting us to help her with supper. Hot potato soup and biscuits. I couldn't help but think, "Oh, Liz, you're a lifesaver! If we had still been on our own, we never would have survived this!"

After supper, Liz got us kids practicing for the concert, first by singing, which cheered us up and got us in the Christmas mood. When Roy felt perkier, we asked if he had his lines for Hec in with his school books. He said they were upstairs on the dresser so I ran up there. Sure enough, there they were, handwritten by Miss Locken on long sheets of foolscap. I said Louise's part, and also my own, acting as the naughty child, which gave Roy a chance to have the same practice he would have had at school. The play put us all in a giddy mood. We were sheltered and warm inside, even though the frightful storm wailed and rattled at the door.

Will asked Dad, "Will it be over in the morning?"

Dad said maybe it would blow itself out in the night, and that we could only hope it would. It seemed odd to have the dog in the house, as he was always an outside dog. Skipper lay contentedly by the heater, and made no protest about being inside. Animals know.

Dad turned on the radio for weather reports and warnings. They were looking for an RCMP officer near the city who was missing, probably stuck in the whiteout on a country road. It was so easy to lose your way in a blizzard like this. The violent wind made strange sounds that I'd never heard before. I looked around the room, thankful that all seven of us were safe and warm on such a treacherous night.

MY ELEVENTH BIRTHDAY

I had a hunch the storm had stolen my birthday. I decided not to mention it, because likely with the blizzard still raging, everyone else would have forgotten I would be eleven when I woke up in the morning. I was wrong again. I had underestimated my family. I woke up to the sound of their voices below. I pulled on my blue sweater over my pajamas and put on extra socks, and rushed downstairs. There it was – a two-layer birthday cake in the middle of the white tablecloth with eleven candles on it.

"Happy birthday, Dot!" That was from Nicky.

"That cake is there for show," Liz said, "It's for supper, not breakfast. I already wrote the recipe for chocolate cake in your book."

Liz must have baked it last night after I went to bed. What a woman!

"Thank you, Liz."

She made a generous pot of porridge and we all sat down to breakfast together. Before we ate, Dad handed me a package. Of course he didn't say anything, but it was obvious. It had to be a birthday gift. Liz planned ahead when they sent the Eaton's order. Of all the games and toys that were shown in the Christmas wish book, she couldn't have chosen better. It was a Bingo game, perfect for passing time, as the blizzard was still howling, and it looked like another day at home.

When Dad and the older boys ventured outside to do the necessary chores, we worried till they were safely back in the house. As they opened the door to go out, we had a peek at the fury of the storm. For those few moments, the wind blasted snow inside the kitchen, and a cloud of white, frigid air chilled the whole house.

It was a memorable birthday, the best in my memory. In the afternoon *Let's Go West* was on the radio as usual. Liz sang along with the familiar songs, which was most of them. The chocolate cake was slathered with caramel icing that I loved. Inside the cake Liz had hidden money - nickels and lots of pennies, and a button. She had Mac and Nick wrap the coins and the "bachelor button" in waxed paper before I came downstairs in the morning. Whoever got the button was supposed to be unmarried for life, and guess who got it? Dad! There was an awkward silence as he unwrapped the waxed paper, and held up the bright, red button. I blew out the candles, and wondered what my new year held for me. After supper, the whole family played Bingo, and Liz was the caller. "Under the B, 10." Mac was helping her and repeating, "Under the B, 10. Under the O, 60." It was reassuring to hear him pronounce all those words. I went to bed happy.

AFTER THE STORM

I t turned out to be a three-day blizzard, December 12th to the 14th. The amount of snow was mind-boggling. When the weather finally settled down, Dad shoveled for ages, to make a path to the chicken house. He managed to find where the door should be, and shoveled some more, enough to pry it open. The chickens were in a pile. The question was whether they had smothered each other. Will was behind Dad, with a pail of warm water, and a full pot of oatmeal porridge Liz sent along for the hens. Upon inspection, it was determined they had survived in their igloo!

On Friday, there was a noisy commotion as tractors and snowplows pushed their way into our yard, shoving back the snow into towering piles. The boys and Dad had to shovel our cutter out of the snowbank, as it had been completely covered over by the swirling snow. When we finally returned to school, the cutter sloped this way and that as the snowdrifts were high on parts of the road, even though the plows had come through and done their best.

As school began, Miss Locken announced, "This will go down in history as one of Saskatchewan's worst storm - the blizzard of '55. You won't forget it, and you will tell your children about it someday."

We then spent the morning sharing stories of how we had survived. Some students went across the road to the Miller farm and stayed there overnight, because their parents couldn't get through. Mrs. Miller played Twenty Questions with them, and Chinese checkers, and found places for them all to sleep.

Miss Locken commented she was thankful the Turners insisted she go home with them, rather than stay in her teacherage alone. Edith said her dad wouldn't leave until all the children were on their way. By then, the storm was raging, and they could see nothing ahead or behind them. Not one of the three of them -Bud, Miss Locken, or Edith - had any sense of direction, but the team of Clydesdales knew very well where they were going. The horses pulled out of the schoolyard, turned north, and took them straight into Turner's yard.

Louise Bell related her story of her Dad getting lost for a couple of hours the second day, between the barn and the house. Then came stories of how other families, like us, had secured a rope to the house to help guide them back. Roy said he froze his cheeks. When most of the students had shared something of their experience, Miss Locken looked in my direction, "What about you, Dorothy?" I was quick to answer. "Tuesday was my birthday, and it was a perfect day!"

THE CHRISTMAS CONCERT

When we practiced our lines for the concert, I could tell Miss Locken noticed that our family didn't miss a word. And we sang the songs louder and better than the rest, as we were sure of the words and the tune. She probably guessed what we had been doing during the storm.

The Christmas concert was scheduled for Dec 21st, and we were all hoping the weather would be fine, so we could go ahead with it. Mr. Turner came on the Monday, and got the older boys to help him put in the stage. Mike Miller from across the road helped, too. The stage was in three parts, joined together to make a raised platform for our program. The hooks that had been on the walls all year, now had a purpose. Dark green curtains were strung with wire across the front of the stage, and the ends of the wires fastened to the wall hooks. The curtains changed the look of our schoolroom, and so did the red and green crepe paper streamers. A couple of days later, Mr. Turner showed up with a Christmas tree, and a four-gallon crock full of sand, probably from his cellar, to place it in. He was a bit of a hero since last year's altercation with Bob Walker. He also took care of things at the school, like putting in the stage, setting up the tree, and making sure Miss Locken was okay. All of the girls from Grade 4 and up carefully decorated the tree to perfection, with bells and balls and tinsel, and an elegant, pointy glass tree topper.

The night of the concert was cold, but clear. Liz had been busy at the sewing machine all that week, and when it came time to get dressed for the concert, we all looked more than presentable. We were dolled up! Liz trimmed my bangs so they were the perfect length. The night before the concert, I heard her quietly talking to Roy, and then there he was, with the haircutting cape around his shoulders, and the yellow barber kit box on the table. She cut his hair, shaping it on the sides, and cutting it shorter at the back. Roy held a mirror so he could supervise every snip, and at the end, Liz said he looked like a prince. I was positive Louise Bell would be impressed when Hec said it!

Parents and friends packed into our small schoolroom. The stage took up a lot of the room, but somehow people sat close together on benches or stood at the back. To start the program, the curtains were partially opened, wide enough for Bud Turner to stand at the front of the stage, and welcome everyone. He opened the program with these words, "Miss Locken and her students have been practicing for weeks. Hang on to your hats, folks! It's going to be a grand show!"

The quilt draw was next. They announced that Santa would come at the end, and they thought they should get the raffle draw out of the way at the beginning. Four of the quilting ladies came to the front, and unfolded the prize. They held it up for all to see, and it was as pretty as a picture. I could see our block with the words, "The Cleaver Family", arched across it in bright red. The quilters had placed it in the middle. We had sold books of tickets to whoever would buy them - ten cents a ticket, or three for twenty-five. Liz bought quite a few, and put our names on them. Mrs. Fiske, being one of the quilters, stepped up to make the draw from a metal pail half full of tickets. Doris Miller held the pail while two ladies carefully folded the quilt, and put it back in the cardboard box. Everyone was leaning forward for the draw as Mrs. Fiske fluffed up the tickets in the pail, and dug deep to the bottom. She pulled one out, and handed it to Mrs. Miller to read the lucky winner's name. Silence. Then, "Roy Cleaver! Congratulations!" Roy stood up and shook his head. "But I didn't buy a ticket." I was proud of him for being honest.

"Go on up there," Mr. Fiske said, giving Roy a push. "Somebody else bought one for you, and put your name on it." Roy went to the front, looking his best. He was getting taller, growing into a man. He wore a white shirt. How Liz managed that, I do not know. The crowd was clapping. Roy came back towards his seat, carrying the box. He leaned into the row where I was sitting, and placed the box on my knee. "It's all yours, little sister!"

I couldn't believe it. This was too much. The special, beautiful, wonderful quilt with "The Cleaver Family" on it was mine? I shook my head. The look on Maxine's face was pure jealousy. Louise poked me in the back. "Lucky you, Dot!"

The concert got even better from there. The Grade Ones opened with a welcome recitation. All the items on the program went smoothly, without a hitch. The green curtains were opened and closed, as whispers and running feet were heard between the different items on the program. The *Hec Says It* play was the crowning glory of the evening. At the very end, all of us who had been in the play ran onto the stage, lined up in a straight row, and shouted, "Hec said it!" Roy grabbed Louise's hand, and they took a deep bow. The clapping was thunderous!

Then Miss Locken was called to the stage, and given a box of chocolates by Bud Turner. She attempted to wish everyone a Merry Christmas and a Happy New Year, but suddenly there was a boisterous commotion at the back of the room. The sound of stamping feet, the loudest voice you can imagine—"Ho-ho-ho!", along with the jingle of sleigh bells. It was almost more than we could take. Little Mac was standing on Liz's lap yelling, "ho-ho-ho" and people were laughing at him because he was so pudgy, like a miniature Santa himself. The school board members handed out a brown paper bag to every child present, even if they were from another school. The bags held peanuts, candy, and a Christmas orange. As if that wasn't enough, every student and preschooler was given a gift, bought from the proceeds of the quilt raffle as well as a donation from the school board. The gifts had been ordered from Eaton's. The teacher simply sent in a list of all sixteen students, whether they were male or female, and their ages, so the staff at the mail-order office could choose suitable gifts. Mine had a typewritten tag on it - "Girl, age 11". I was thrilled with my foam rubber Bugs Bunny toy that had wires inside, so I could twist him into crazy positions.

It was snowing when we left the school, and rode home in the cutter. Because Liz and Mac were with us, we were stuffed in there like sardines in a can. Nick sat on Liz's lap, and Mac sat on me. The quilt box was beside Liz. I trusted her to take care of it. We talked all the way home about how spectacular it was. Liz couldn't praise us enough, and told us over and over how proud she was. We ate the candy from our candy bags, and gave Dad all the licorice, as most of us didn't like it anyway.

When Liz and I went up to our bedroom, she said, "Come on, Dot! Let's celebrate the night by sleeping under this fabulous quilt!"

We spread it out, and even though it was late, I wanted to check each block. It was so interesting to see what each person had chosen for their design—birds, butterflies, roses. I would be spending a lot of time in the days to come figuring out who embroidered which block. This quilt was precisely what the letter had promised – a community treasure.

I called Roy into our room to show him how it looked. He could tell I loved it. He grinned, his long curls a little askew from wearing his toque on the way home. I believed ever since Mom died that we were a rag-tag, looked-down-on family. Somehow tonight erased all that. I heard numerous comments about our acting, and how well dressed we were. As we cuddled up under the exquisite quilt, Liz said, "Boy, did those Cleaver kids ever shine tonight!"

AND THEN THERE
WAS CHRISTMAS!

The storm, my birthday, the quilt, the concert - so many over the top, unforgettable events. I could hardly believe we would still have Christmas on top of all that! The Christmas concert was the last time we would be at the school in 1955. School would resume after the New Year.

With a few days till Christmas, our house was again buzzing with excitement and preparation. The blizzard seemed to trigger smaller storms for the rest of the winter. I overheard Stan Bell tell Dad he couldn't remember such a miserable, cold winter with one storm right on the heels of the last one. Almost every day brought wind and snow and frigid temperatures. I dreaded going out each day to get wood, as filling the wood box continued to be the main job for Nick and me. We begged Liz to make blizzard masks for us, and she did, which helped to keep the cold from numbing my forehead and my nose. Inside, Liz enlisted our help to make gingersnaps and shortbread cookies, and she talked a lot about all the things we would have on the table for Christmas dinner. She planned to make banana cream pies, and so, on the 24th, Dad set out for town with the team and cutter, to buy bananas and last-minute items. The roads were still heavy with snow, even though the V-ploughs were out each day. Will rode along with Dad, and he said the horses turned off the road and into the stubble fields, where the snow wasn't as deep. They were called field roads, and the horses picked the best way through.

On Christmas Day, I felt we finally had the dream family I had longed for since Mom left us. Dad talked more than usual, and Liz, of course, talked all the time. Dad and Mac had a nap after we ate, and the rest of us helped with dishes, tidied up the house, and checked out our presents.

In the afternoon we played a couple of rounds of Bingo. Then Dad moved the table across the kitchen floor, until it was directly under a square panel in the ceiling. The panel covered the hole to the attic, and by standing on the table, Dad was able to push it out of the way, and hoist himself up into the dark space above. He disappeared from our view, except for his long, dangling legs. In a couple of minutes, he handed down a square board that turned out to be a crokinole game, and then tossed down a drawstring bag of wooden disks to complete the game. We wasted no time getting a game going. Four could play at once. Will and I, as usual, were partners. We were making 20's like crazy after a few practice shots. Dad played with us, and he was an expert, even though he probably hadn't played for years.

The little boys weren't quite old enough to play well, and to make them happy, resourceful Liz converted her trusty deck of solitaire cards into a game of Old Maid. She simply removed all the face cards and the aces, leaving numbered cards and the Queen of Spades. The game was played a lot like Go Fish, matching pairs, and was excellent practice for Nick and Mac to work with numbers. The players kept drawing cards from the others and making matching pairs. Whoever got stuck with the Old Maid, the Queen of Spades, was the loser.

At the end of the day, Liz challenged anyone brave enough to face her in crokinole. We hadn't even considered that she might want to play. She beat all of us kids, and called us losers. Dad said he could finish her off in three rounds, but he was mistaken. It seemed he had lost his touch from winning in the afternoon games. Liz laughed when she won, and called him a loser, too.

The days after Christmas were relaxed around home. Liz taught Will how to use the sewing machine, which was quite a trick to pedal evenly with your feet, while guiding the cloth with your hands, and steering clear of the needle. It was fun to watch him. The snow piled up in the yard, a little more every day. The drifts were hard as a rock.

A NEW YEAR BEGINNING

January 1956

It was around New Year's Day that Liz went downhill. I noticed tears well up in her eyes for no particular reason and I felt a nagging fear that our lives were about to change once again. She seemed tired, and often went to her room. I thought maybe we had tired her out too much with all the work and excitement of getting us through the storm, my special birthday, the concert, and our family Christmas. I hoped if she took it easy, and maybe took an afternoon nap each day, she would get her old zip back.

I knew Liz best, because we shared the upstairs bedroom. When I was freezing at night, she often cuddled me up, and sometimes she said things like, "Dot, I had a girl like you once." I had always been curious about where Liz had lived and if she had a family.

"Where is your girl now?"

"She doesn't love me," Liz answered in the dark. "She says I ruined her life." I didn't know what to say, so I said what came to my mind at the moment.

"I don't think you could ruin anyone's life. You did the opposite for me." I could hear her crying softly beside me.

"You gave us a perfect Christmas!" Liz reached for my hand and finally, we both fell asleep.

In the following days, her low became lower. Where was the fun and silly lady who made faces behind Dad's back when she poured his coffee? It all came to an end on January 8. The moon was full, and when I woke up in the middle of the night, Liz was not there. I looked out the window, way down at the farmyard, bathed in bright moonlight. Sure enough, there was Liz. She was wearing her winter boots, thank goodness, but her red coat was wide open in the freezing wind. She was desperately pounding on the door of the barn, and then the chicken house, as if some unseen hand had locked them against her.

That was it. Dad must have contacted her relatives or the police, and Liz was gone. We came home from school once again to the familiar, empty house. Breakfast dishes were still on the table, and the fire was low. It was now my job to get wood in the stove, and water in the dishpan, but I stood there in the kitchen, seeing all that empty space. Liz should have been there, with her toothy grin and some smart comment. Dad came into the house to warm up, and Will asked him, "Is Liz okay?" Dad avoided looking at me, as he shrugged his shoulders and said, "As okay as she'll ever be, I guess."

I quietly spoke to Will, as I went upstairs, "I'm not coming down."

Dear old Dad could have his bedroom back tomorrow, not tonight. Dear old Dad could cook supper. How about that? I shut the bedroom door, and wedged a chair under the doorknob. It was a perfect way to lock everyone out. I curled up in the blankets of the unmade bed. That's when I heard the crinkle of paper. I felt around under the pillows. There it was - a note, in that same loopy handwriting in my birthday recipe book.

"Dear little Dot". Liz knew I liked being called that. She didn't write the word "Dot". She put a tiny black dot in place of my name. Tears were blurring the letter, but I blinked to see what she had to say. It was short.

"Hold on to your dreams. Love, Liz." She made one loopy "L" for both words "Love" and "Liz". Oh, my heart! I cried so much, huddled under my beautiful quilt. I could hear the family moving around below, but I wasn't going downstairs, not for any money. I think I fell asleep for a while. Later, I heard the boys come up to their bedroom next door. I waited. I planned to sneak out to the outhouse after the house was quiet. No rush. I wasn't even hungry, but I did have to "go".

Finally, I quietly removed the chair that held the door, and tip-toed down the stairs. The clouds had covered most of the dark sky, but there was still faint moonlight shining in the windows. I went past Dad. He never slept on my little cot under the stairs, as he was too tall, so he used the click-clack couch in the living room. If you pulled the seat upwards till you heard a click, then it opened up like magic, into a flat bed.

I grabbed my jacket from the coat hooks by the door and stuffed my feet in a pair of boots, probably Will's. Outside, the air was killer cold. Faithful old Skipper left his straw bed in the doghouse beside the step, and trotted to my side. We made the trip to the outhouse together, and on the way back, I heard the lonely howl of a coyote far away. Skipper's fur bristled around his neck and I was glad he was with me.

As I closed the door, and slipped off my jacket, I could see Dad lying on his back, his elbow stuck out to the side, and his hand under his head. I silently went towards the stairs.

"Dot."

I stopped. Whatever he had to say, there was a little fire left in me. I was ready.

"Yeah."

"Don't blame me. She was crazy as a loon. She had to go." I couldn't remember the last time he had talked to me, directly to me, and I felt the fire in me drain away.

"Well, she was nicer to me in four months than you've ever been in 11 years." I don't know where that came from, but it was as if I had been waiting to say it. I didn't think he was going to say anything else, but he did. He didn't move, or look at me. He kept staring at the ceiling. "I figure to do better with that."

Part of me wanted to tear into him, and the other part of me was just sad, sad, and more sad.

I said, "Okay." I said it, softly. Maybe he heard, and maybe he didn't.

BACK TO SCHOOL

I was eager to go back to school, even though there would be long, tippy cutter rides on the field roads. The concert had been such a highlight. I wondered if Miss Locken would tell us she was proud of our performance. She did tell us exactly that, saying her parents had come from town for the concert, and they were simply amazed and impressed by all the students. I wish I had known they were there, because it is always interesting to see someone's mother. But thinking back, I was so excited that night, I probably wouldn't have been able to take notice.

Miss Locken asked if anyone knew why December 22nd was special, besides being the beginning of our recent Christmas holidays. None of us knew, so she explained it was officially the first day of winter, and had the least amount of daylight. She asked if we noticed how dark it was when we got up in the mornings, and how quickly the light faded in the afternoon. The best news, she explained, was that from the 22nd onward, the daylight was getting a wee bit longer, till finally in springtime we would have lots of sunshine.

As I expected, Miss Locken had some plans for the new school year. She had printed "Happy New Year" on the blackboard as well as a poem for the month. It was another by Helen Hunt Jackson, called "New Year's Morning". I learned it by heart before the day was over. The last verse was my favorite; I loved how the words went together.

> Only a night from old to new;
> Only a sleep from night to morn.
> The new is but the old come true;
> Each sunrise sees a new year born.

Somehow, even though Liz was gone, I had a little seed of hope in my heart that this New Year was going to be special. Last year was all about losing Mom, and 1956 felt like a fresh start, with promise for better things ahead.

Miss Locken asked if any of us had a crokinole board at home. There were two boards at school. We needed two more, so all 16 students could play at once, four to a board, when the weather was too cold and stormy to go outside. Roy offered to bring ours, and Edith Turner said they had one to loan as well.

Even the thought of crokinole at school was exciting, and we practiced all evening at home, so we could make a fair showing the next day. But it was not to be. When we woke up, the wind was howling, and the temperature had plunged to minus 44. Dad called it a home day, so at least we had another day to practice crokinole. We tried our other games, but somehow without Liz, the day was flat.

I remembered the canned chicken in the sealers in the cellar, and Will helped make a tasty supper. We put the chicken in a roaster in the oven, along with carrots, potatoes, and onions. At the last minute, I grabbed my recipe book and turned to Liz's writing, "Rich Man's Pudding". Will wasn't much for baking, so I asked him to get the water boiling for the sauce. The batter didn't take long to make. Mom's tin flour bin was always full and at the ready, and I stirred in the sugar, baking powder, raisins, and a pinch of salt. The last step was to melt butter and brown sugar in three cups of boiling water and pour it over the batter. I asked Will to handle that, as the kettle was heavy. There was just enough room to slide the pan into the oven, beside the chicken.

When I saw Liz's writing again, I realized she wanted me to have those recipes so I could bake for the family when she was gone. That was hard. Worst of all, was wondering where she was, and if she was okay.

WHAT IN THE WORLD
IS HAPPENING?

On a Saturday morning, a couple of weeks after Liz disappeared from our lives, Dad finished the morning chores, and put on his "good" clothes. They weren't all that good, but they were different from his chore pants, and his army green parka, with the fur-trimmed hood. It was cold outside, as it had been ever since the three-day storm in December. We knew Dad was going somewhere with the truck, because he fished around in the heater with the coal shovel, for some red-hot coals and put them in a tin pan. When he went outside, Nick and I watched him through a hole in the thick frost on the kitchen window. He shoved the coals under the truck to thaw it out. He put the shovel in the back of the truck, and some blankets, extra mitts, scarf, and his heavy parka on the seat beside him. The weather was a bit better, and the plowed roads were as clear as they had been, since the big storm. He kept going in and out of the house for this and that, and finally managed to fire up the engine. Of course, he left it running so it wouldn't give up while he came in one last time to tell Roy what chores needed to be done in the afternoon. He said he'd be back for milking. I guess we were all scared of him, or we would have asked where he was going. As soon as he left, Roy cranked up the radio. It was tuned to the station Liz liked and at that moment, Elvis was singing, "That's Alright Mama."

We kept the fire going, and fooled around all afternoon. If we had known what was happening that day, we would have been a little on edge. As far as we understood, it was merely another winter day on the weekend, with not a lot to do. Nick and I made a batch of Rickety Uncles, and we played Snakes and Ladders at the table, while

Mac took a little nap. For supper, I heated a couple of cans of tomato soup and made some toast.

It wasn't that late, but it was pitch dark when we heard the old truck come into the lane. As Miss Locken had explained, winter is a dark time on the prairie with few hours of daylight. When I heard the noise, I jumped up, and turned on the yard light. I could see the truck swerve a bit on the lane. The snow was fairly deep, and Dad had to keep up the speed or he'd be stuck. For a moment, I was silly enough to think maybe he brought us a treat. Well, he brought us something, all right, but it wasn't exactly a treat!

The door opened, and with a blast of frosty air, in walked a person - a kid or a woman, I didn't know. She had a mane of red hair, and wore a shabby brown coat. Another housekeeper! Wow, why did he always keep us in the dark? Dad was behind her, carrying her suitcase. He stared at us as we were gaping at them, and said, "This is Maggie. We got married."

What the heck! Married? Dad turned around, and without a word went outside. Coward! She was scared to death, looking from side to side at the kitchen, like a caged bird. I wondered what she thought of our not-so-fancy house. The crooked, green cupboard in the corner, the chipped cups on the table, and the smell of burned tomato soup in the air. She stood by the window that faced the barn. The panes were covered with thick frost, except for a little hole we had chipped away to see out. I guessed she was watching for Dad.

Roy said the same thing he did when Liz showed up unexpectedly. "It's chore time." We had been lazy all afternoon. There was wood to get in, and the older boys still had to milk the cows. Nick and I started clearing the table, and chubby, little Mac grabbed a cup, and held it up to the dishpan on the stove.

I looked at Maggie's back. She still hadn't taken off her coat. I couldn't tell how old she was. She looked young. Why would she marry a man with five kids? Didn't she know how much work we were? Would the craziness ever end?

Will had already gone to the barn, but Roy was at the door when I went out for wood. He walked with me to the woodpile, and we both loaded up. I asked him if he had known anything about this, and he said, "No, of course not."

I asked Roy, "How long do you think Dad had this planned? You can't find a wife in a day!"

Roy shook his head. His nose was red with cold, and his toque was pulled down to his eyebrows.

"He's nuts, Dot! We pulled the short straw when we got him for a dad."

I felt tears welling up, but Roy wouldn't know, because I could fool him with the cold. It made both our eyes water. "I wish Liz was still here."

He smiled, and said, "Yeah. Liz was all right!"

"What do we do now, Roy?"

We had reached the outside wood box by the kitchen door, and Roy dumped his heavy armload of stove wood sticks into it. "Soon as we're old enough, little sister, we run away from home."

I carried my wood inside, and dropped it on the floor by the stove. It would be a cold night, and the stove had an endless gut. Maggie had whipped up the few dishes, and was wiping off the table. Nick had almost finished putting the dishes away. When I saw that, I guessed she had an idea how to work. All I could think of was Dad holding up the red, bachelor button from my birthday cake! Unmarried for life! Ha! That sure didn't last long!

Maggie didn't talk much, so she and Dad made quite a pair! She was always on the move, and kept busy with cleaning and dishes. On Monday, she did the wash. Clothes that had been frozen crisp and cold on the line outside, earlier in the day, were hanging neatly on the lines strung up on hooks in the living room. The lines were taken down the next day and put away. I wonder how Maggie had found them and managed a wash day on her own, only two days after she arrived. She must have opened her mouth for a change, and asked Dad. A cook, she was not! She burned stuff more than I did, which made me more thankful than ever for the recipe book Liz had written out for me.

Months later, I asked Maggie why she hardly ever talked. She answered sharply, "I'll talk when I have something say." So, I guess she didn't have anything to say yet, as she silently worked around the house as the weeks went by. I was curious how she treated Mac when we were gone to school. I wondered if she talked to him, or if she ignored him. He came running to me every day when I came through the door, and his usual greeting was "Dottie, play with me!"

As always, I had a thousand questions and not one answer. Days are short in winter on the prairies. By the time we got home from school each afternoon, the pale sun was sinking low in the west and there was enough time for chores, something to eat, and bed. Of course, I was back on my cot in my spot under the stairs. The wife slept upstairs with Dad.

VALENTINES AND THE NORTHERN LIGHTS

February 1956

One night, when the boys came in from milking, Roy said, "Get the little kids and come out." Grabbing my coat and boots, I looked out the door. The northern lights were dancing, pink and green, and yellow. I was impressed that Maggie showed an interest. She pulled on her coat, helped Nick and Mac with theirs, and brought the boys outside. We stood there freezing for a few minutes, spellbound by the swirling, twirling curtains of color. Dad came past us carrying the last pail of milk to the separator. "What's up?"

"Aurora borealis!" Nick yelled out.

Dad turned and glanced up at the light show. He ruffled Nick's hair. "Aren't you getting smart these days, Mr. Grade One!" Sad how thrilled Nick was to have Dad give him a few kinds words!

It was important to me that Nick and I continued to get 100% on our Friday spelling words, even though Liz was no longer with us. We practiced Thursday nights, but the fun had gone out of it. I didn't even try to make up the silly sentences, as she had done, to explain the meaning of the words. Nick was smart, and did well in all the school subjects. It seemed after our brilliant participation at the concert, the others treated us better. Adele and Maxine were nicer to me, and I felt included. That means a lot when you are eleven years old!

And so, the month of February unfolded, with each day gaining a bit of daylight. Miss Locken planned a Valentine's party, and invited all preschoolers in the district to join us. I wondered if Maggie would come, and bring Mac. He was now four years old and I was sure he would love to come to school. We decorated the schoolroom with hearts and crepe paper streamers. Louise and Edith fancied up a cardboard box with red paper and ribbons to collect all the valentines we would give to each other.

We had a problem at home that night. We were, of course, expected to exchange valentines with the other students, but we hadn't bought any. Liz would have come up with something, but this time we were stuck. After supper, Maggie handed us two books of push-out valentines. They were fancy ones, too. She said it popped into her mind when she was in town with Dad and Mac, and luckily, they still had some at Fletcher's Store. The next hour was spent choosing which valentines we would give to which friends. Roy picked out a couple for Louise and Edith. I wondered if Bully Bob would get even one card! Nick grabbed all the ones with animals on them. Maggie told us not to forget to each give one to the teacher, so she would give us better marks. That wasn't how things worked with Miss Locken, but Maggie didn't know much about that. The important thing was that she had come through for us with those special valentines, and we were grateful.

Maggie arrived with Mac at two o'clock for the party. As soon as they came in the door, Mac came running to me. Even though he was a chunky kid, I picked him up for a few minutes, and then led him around, introducing him to some of my friends, and letting him sit with me at my desk. Maxine came over to me, pointed to Maggie, and asked, "Is that your mom?"

I didn't take long to answer. "Nope, she sure is not!"

One day at school, I found Nick sitting at his desk during recess. I asked if he was feeling okay, as all the students were outside and I was heading out there myself. The whole school was making a snow fort, as the snowdrifts were ideal for cutting snow blocks. The other two six year old boys in the school had chummed up and Nick was left out. I remembered something Liz had said. I repeated it to Nick which made him smile, "I'll tell you what, Dot, two is company, three's a crowd. That means three kids don't get along so well. Someone is always left out."

Of course, this would pass, and the trio of boys would be pals again, but I also saw Nick almost in tears sitting at his desk. Such a little nature scientist - I didn't have to search long until I found the right book. It was a bird book with colored pictures. Nick and I sat on the floor by the small bookshelf. We were in the middle of the book, when the two Grade 1 boys came inside because they were cold. As soon as they got their coats off, they came to see what Nick and I were doing.

"Can we look, too?" I looked at them both, and narrowed my eyes. "Yes, you can, but don't you ever try to cut Nick out again."

They promised they never would, and we moved over so they could join us, as I read aloud about the tiny ruby-throated hummingbirds that can fly 30 miles an hour, all the way to Mexico for the winter. I had put those Grade 1 boys on notice that the Cleavers are a proud family, and we stick together.

THE BULLY STRIKES AGAIN

March 1956

The contrast was too much. Liz used to talk all the time and Maggie wouldn't talk at all! It was impossible to get to know her, and things were quiet at home.

School was our happy place that winter, and Miss Locken held the students' interest with completing the 3 R's each day, which she jokingly called Readin', Ritin' and Rithmetic. She also planned some extras. There was a new health program that came to our district, which included posters to tack on the school walls, with a colored picture and a few words. One of them said, "When you cough or sneeze or sniff, Do it in your handkerchief." The additional signs were about brushing teeth, washing hands, getting fresh air, exercise, drinking water and milk, and eating healthy food. The issue of exercise and fresh air was no problem for us. If it was too cold to go outside at school, we certainly got enough of both at home, doing our chores.

Miss Locken had us each make a chart, and check off the health items each day in February. We all were aware it was the shortest month, but as we drew the lines for our chart someone asked if February had 28 or 29 days this year. I noticed Miss Locken took every opportunity to teach us something. She asked the whole school, "How do we know if 1956 will be a leap year with 29 days in February?" No one came up with the answer, so she wrote on the board 1956 divided by four. She invited some of the older kids to go to the board and do the arithmetic. She asked them, "Does four go into it evenly, with no remainder?" The students worked out the numbers while we watched, and of course, Will quickly came up with the answer. "Yes, Miss Locken, it does go evenly - 489."

"Okay, so we do have a leap year. Put 29 days on your chart." As we helped the little kids draw the lines with a pencil and ruler to make their charts, she told us about Sadie Hawkins dances held on leap years, when a girl can ask a guy for a date. She said a leap year is the time a woman is allowed to ask a man to marry her. Of course, we immediately thought of Dad and Maggie. Maybe she had asked Dad to marry her, but I highly doubted that, as she would have to open her mouth to say it!

Sometime during March, we had some excitement that no one anticipated. We were having a pleasant day at school, the sun was shining, and finally, we had a day that was not quite so cold. Roy wasn't at school that day, and was sorry that he missed the fun, when he heard about it later. It wasn't exactly fun, especially not for Miss Locken. At exactly 2:15, when last recess was done, Miss Locken sat at her desk and opened the book she always read to us for 15 minutes towards the end of each day. The book was *Misty of Chincoteague* by Marguerite Henry, and all the students were loving it. Nothing better than a horse story! Lily, the lone Grade 6, stood on the school steps, and rang the bell long and loud.

After a few minutes, it was obvious that some of the little boys had not come inside, including Nick. Will and I looked at each other, puzzled, but Miss Locken quickly put two and two together. All the girls were present. Missing were Bully Bob and some of the younger boys. Miss Locken asked Edith to watch the class, while she pulled on her coat and boots. I was proud to see Will get up without being asked, and grab his coat. We heard our teacher say to Will, as they stepped outside, "I know who's behind this!" We could see them walking single file down the skinny, shoveled path to the barn. There were no horses out there, as throughout the winter, all of the students were brought to school by their parents, due to the roads being so heavy with snow. Sometimes, kids went into the barn during the noon hour or recess. The older boys often had a smoke, and thought they were pulling the wool over Miss Locken's eyes. She told them once when they came back in, that she knew very well what they were up to, and they smelled like an ash pail.

The school had a bank of windows on each side. We all ran to the west wall to watch, and Will filled me in later on more details. We watched Miss Locken knock on the barn door.

Louise said, "I bet Bob's got it locked from the inside." The teacher and Will banged on the door at the same time. Immediately, Edith ran to the phone at the back of the room and cranked her home number, one long, three shorts. "Hello, Dad, trouble at the school," and she hung up. In a minute, we saw the barn door open. The younger boys came running out, all four of them trying to hang on to Miss Locken's hands. I imagined they were scared, and maybe crying, and I was worried about Nick. He was still tender-hearted about us losing Liz, and this trauma wasn't going to help. Will and Miss Locken herded the little boys along the path, and sauntering along behind at the tail end, was Mr. Bully himself. Of course, we were all on Miss Locken's side, and were worried about our little brothers. When they entered the school, Nick ran to me and I put my arm tight around him. Bob stayed outside. Every one of us ran to the other side of the room that was also lined with windows to see what would happen next. Nick stayed close to my side.

The road had been freshly plowed, and sure enough, that very welcome, little black coupe that we remembered oh so well from last year, sped into the schoolyard. At the sight of the car, Bob hustled inside and quickly sat down at his desk, looking straight ahead, as if nothing had happened. From the back of the room we heard Bud Turner's deep voice, "What's the problem here?"

Miss Locken held no secrets. "Bob locked the younger boys in the barn and threatened them with a knife!" Our eyes nearly popped out of our heads. A knife! We didn't know about a knife! We found out later it was a small jackknife, but it was enough to terrify the little boys and keep them under his control, scared to escape the barn.

Bud motioned Bob to come outside. He left the door open, and we heard every word. The classroom was perfectly quiet; we didn't want to miss a thing. This was huge.

Mr. Turner spoke first, "Okay Bob, what do you have to say for yourself?"

"Nothing happened, Mr. Turner. I was only having a little fun." Silence. We didn't breathe.

Bud roared, "You call that fun? Terrorizing little kids? You're done here, Bob Walker! We don't tolerate bullying in this school. Never have and never will!"

Bob was feeling feisty apparently, probably because he was on his last leg. There was nothing to lose now.

"Don`t you have to call a meeting of your fancy school board before you can kick me out?" Bob's uncle was on the board, and had been for years.

Mr. Turner continued, "Not this time. You gave us trouble last year, and we agreed then, you're on your face."

Bob wasn't giving up. "You better check with my uncle."

Bud Turner spoke in a loud, even voice. "I don't need to check with your uncle, or with the board, or with the Queen of England. But you know what, I could contact the police, and I've a good mind to do just that. You threatened students with a knife! Have you ever heard of reform school, boy?"

Silence. The smart answers were no more. We had all heard grim stories of reform school. No doubt Bully Bob had, too.

"You better get your coat and boot it for home, Bob. It will give you a chance to cool off."

Mr. Turner came back inside the schoolroom. "It's all under control, kids. The bullying in this school is over!"

Brave little Miss Locken was shaking. Bud sat down on a chair at the back of the room near the door, as if protecting us all. He folded his arms over his chest, and crossed his legs. Miss Locken took a minute to breathe, and then managed a smile.

"Okay class, get comfortable. Let's make a circle with our desks, and we'll take the time we need to finish *Misty of Chincoteague*.

And that is exactly what we did. We sat in our desks, some of us with our little brothers beside us, and she read to us for the next hour till it was time for school to be dismissed. Mr. Turner stuck with us until our parents arrived to take us home.

SIGNS OF SPRING

April 1956

Maggie ordered garden seeds from the Stokes Seed catalog. She asked what kinds of flowers I liked, because she was going to order flower seeds, too. I said, "Violets!", and she said they didn't come in seeds. I suggested the bright yellow and orange California poppies. She ordered a package, and said they would be mine, and I could plant them wherever I wanted to. She said she was a whole lot better at gardening than she was at cooking. We hoped the seeds would come in lots of time, but we need not have worried. There was no danger of them being late, as the winter was not in a hurry to leave. There was so much snow to melt. By the end of the winter, a record snowfall was announced on the radio - 77 inches of snow had fallen in the 1955-56 winter season. That was the same as 6 feet, 5 inches - taller than Dad, if it was all piled up at once.

One morning, I woke up with a painful sore throat. I instantly remembered how sick Nick was when we had to get the nurse to come and stay with us. I told Maggie, and she said to stay home from school and sleep it off. She also said I should drink a lot of water, so I did. From my little area under the stairs on my cot, I watched her do up the morning work, wash the separator, and the dishes. I felt guilty for not helping her.

Before noon, she went upstairs, and came down with a book in her hand. She offered it to me saying, "If you feel well enough to read, this is a suitable book for a girl your age." It was called *An Old-Fashioned Girl*, by Louisa May Alcott, the author of *Little Women*. I had read and loved that book from the bookshelf at school.

"How come you have it here? Did you bring it from home?"

"I did," she answered. "Your Dad told me he had an 11-year-old girl."

Well, that sounded hopeful. I wondered if Maggie had intended to be my friend back when they got married, but I wrecked it all by being mean, and unwelcoming. I opened the book. "Chapter 1, Polly Arrives". I was hooked from the first page, and through to the budding romance between Polly and Tom. Maggie was right. It was a fine story for a girl my age. I lay on my cot under my beautiful quilt, and read till the boys came home from school. I felt better by then, too. I guess the sore throat wasn't serious, as two days later I was back where I liked to be, in my desk by the windows, last seat.

People were calling it a late spring, but as the days went by, the banks of snow slowly, but surely, melted away. We dug out our rubber boots from a box in the porch, because it was too muddy to wear shoes, and too wet for snow boots. In the second week of April, the cawing of the crows proved spring had arrived. It would be awhile till I would hear my favorite bird, the meadowlark. They would bide their time coming back to our cold climate. Soon the pussy willows appeared, mostly in the willows circling the sloughs that were full to the brim with melted runoff. Crocuses would be the first wildflowers to show up. There was a hill in our pasture where they always grew, thick and pale purple in the sun, with tiny bugs in them. Miss Locken could hardly keep up with the "Signs of Spring" list on the blackboard, as she attempted to include all our daily observations. The (now) 15 students of Briar Rose School had a bad case of spring fever. We had been cooped up too long!

Finally, the road was dry enough to hook Queenie to the buggy, and off we went to school, happy to leave the cutter at home. The ditches were full of water, but the sandy road was passable again. Frogs sang incessantly, the surest sign of spring.

When we came home from school one afternoon, we saw Maggie running on the road. Her face was red and sweaty, and she looked like she had seen a ghost. Roy pulled back on the lines, and Maggie panted as soon as we were close enough to hear her, "Mac's gone!"

We sat in the buggy while Roy asked Maggie, "When?"

"A few minutes ago. I checked the clothes on the line to see if they were dry, and when I turned around to go back in the house, he was gone."

We weren't sure what to do. "Not in the house?"

"No, I've checked, I've also checked the ditches."

Oh, so that's why she was out on the road. I wondered if she was genuinely scared that Mac was hurt or dead, or was she scared she'd be in trouble for not watching him? Will and I jumped off the buggy and ran for the house. Nick and Maggie quickly walked back to the yard. Nick was calling, "Mac, come back! Mac, come back!" Will and I raced around inside the house, taking a quick look under the beds. You never know with a little kid if they might fall asleep in an unlikely place.

I checked the outhouse, and even looked down the hole. Roy took Queenie to the water trough and then combed the barnyard: henhouse, pigpen, inside the barn, the granary, the straw stacks. We were all getting scared. Maggie looked like death as she ran around with us, calling and searching.

Nick - smart little Nick - asked, "Where's the dog?"

True, we hadn't seen Skipper in our rush to find our brother. Nick had learned to whistle in the last week, and was pleased the dog would come when he heard it. Great idea, Nick! We stood in the lane wondering where to try next. To our relief, when Nick whistled a second time, our fat little brother emerged from the bush south of the house, with his hand on Skipper's back. The dog had brought him home. Maggie sank to the ground, put her head in her hands, and cried. The rest of us ran to Mac, and Roy bawled him out for running away.

After a while, we all settled down and went into the house. Probably Mac hadn't been very far from the house, but he gave us a horrible scare. Hopefully, with Roy's stern words Mac had learned a lesson.

Roy couldn't leave it alone. "Are you gonna stay close to Maggie now?" Mac nodded, his little chin quivering.

I shook my head at my oldest brother. "Leave him alone Roy, he gets it."

That was my first inkling that Maggie was part of us. She did care about Mac, maybe about all of us. I remembered the valentines she bought, and the book she loaned me. Maybe we would someday be a real family again.

SPRING ON THE FARM

May 1956

Maggie's mom came while we were at school so we didn't get to see her. I wondered what her mother would look like. Probably red-haired like Maggie. I had the same thought as I did when I missed seeing Miss Locken's parents at the Christmas concert - "It's interesting to see someone's mother."

Maggie showed us the four nesting boxes she had set in the henhouse, each with a "clucky hen" in it. She told us not to go near them, because the hens were already upset by their move from Maggie's former home. Each hen was sitting on a clutch of eggs. Nick especially marveled at the notion the eggs could turn into live baby chicks.

Maggie explained, "You know they're broody when they won't get off their nest, except to eat and drink at night, when we can't see them." *Broody*. That was a new word to us. It would be fun to see baby chicks around the farm. Maggie said in about 21 days, if things worked out for the hens, there would be some little peeps in our henhouse.

Spring on the farm meant baby animals. Baby pigs, so pink and cute. There was a tiny one that almost didn't look real. He looked like a toy. Dad said he was the runt, and would probably do okay if the bigger piglets didn't push him away from the food. The old sow had given birth to nine babies, and when it was time to feed them, she flopped down on her side and let them go for it.

I told Dad I hated the smell of dirty pigs. He said, "They aren't dirty. They're the only animals on this farm who use one corner of their pen for a toilet. That keeps the rest of their pen nice and clean."

Dad gave the sow lots of straw, and the piglets were fun to watch as they nosed around in it, and then piled up on each other to sleep most of the day. Sleep and eat, that was what they did.

The cows all had calves, and we got to name them. The boys chose uninteresting names like Spot, Blackie, and Red. That didn't bother me. I was waiting for the kittens and I had the best name picked out for mine. The cat had been missing for two days. She always hid them from us, and we had a rule that whoever found them got first pick. As I was drying dishes, I mentioned to Maggie that I wanted to be the one to find the kittens.

She said, "Oh, do you? Well, I know where they are." She sure loved knowing something I didn't.

"Where?"

She grinned. "That's for me to know and for you to find out!"

I was ticked with Maggie for saying that. I had an idea she might go check after we were done our work, to see if they were still there. So often, the mother cat moved the poor little things if she thought her secret was found out. So, I stood near the window spying on Maggie. I thought she was going to the outhouse, but then she veered off to the woodpile and ducked in behind it. I took off as fast as I could. Yep, the mother cat had made a nest under some boards. I stared as hard as I could, as it was dark under there, but oh mercy! There were four kittens. Two were white, and one of them would be mine!

So many spring babies on the farm! At least Skipper wasn't going to have pups, that's for sure. Dad was seeding the crop toward the end of May, as the fields had finally dried up, and he kept Roy out of school to help. There was lots of farm work I didn't take much interest in – disking, harrowing, testing the seed for germination. I left all that worry to Dad and the boys. The crop was important - wheat to sell, oats for feed. I knew that much.

The cattle were plagued by black flies, sometimes the dreadful warble flies, and mosquitoes. As they stood in the barnyard in the evening after milking, Dad often put some wet straw in a couple of piles and lit a match. He called it a smudge. The smoke gave the cattle some relief from the summer insects, as it drifted across the barnyard, and hung in the air.

There were seagulls around the farm, and they followed Dad's machinery in the field. As the machine turned over the soil and exposed grubs and worms, the gulls were quick to help themselves to dinner. A cloud of white gulls in the air behind Dad and his tractor was a common sight.

One particular gull was hanging around the barnyard, and Nick and I tamed it. We were sitting up on the henhouse roof one evening eating some bread, and the gull came closer and closer begging for a bite. We threw him a crust, and that was it. The next night, we were there again and so was he. Being a scavenger, he wasn't fussy about the quality of our offerings. From our perch on the henhouse roof, Nick and I watched him hop closer, and turn his head this way and that, as if to say, "What did you bring tonight?" He came every time, his black beady eyes not on us, but on whatever scrap of food we brought for him.

Each evening when the boys and Dad were milking the cows outside, Nick and I fed our gull, gathered the eggs, and listened for the train. It blew into town every weeknight at about 8 o'clock, and the sound of the lonesome whistle carried a long way, out to our farm five miles away. So often a school poem jumped into my mind. It could happen at any time of the day. I don't know why I liked memorizing so much but when I heard the train, I thought of a poem in our reader, *Up and Away*. The name of the poem was "Travel". Nick liked to hear poetry, so I recited a verse.

> The railroad track is miles away,
> And the day is loud with voices speaking,
> Yet there isn't a train goes by all-day
> But I hear its whistle shrieking.

I told Nick about my dream to take a train trip through the Rocky Mountains, and he asked if I would take him along. I said sure. He was as curious and adventurous as I was. We talked about the railroad track winding up and around the massive mountains, over railway bridges above rushing rivers, and through tunnels that had been blasted with dynamite. Miss Locken told us there was a dining car with fancy meals on the train, and sleeping cars with curtained off beds. So, my little brother and I had a plan. Someday we would find ourselves on the trip of a lifetime "in the blue Canadian Rockies"!

I joined Maggie in her eagerness to plant the garden on the long weekend in May. It was called Victoria Day, always falling on the Monday before May 24th. This year, the Monday fell on May 21st. Dad cultivated the garden patch a couple of times to dig up the dirt, and get rid of the lumps. There was a silly verse that some of the kids at school were saying as we left the school on the Friday of the long weekend.

"The 24th of May is the queen's birthday,
If we don't get a holiday we'll all run away."

I don't think any one of the students at our school would ever want to run away from it. Roy was sorry to be missing school and Miss Locken sent home his math homework and the Grade 8 reader, in case he had time to keep up with it. He would be facing important examinations at the end of June.

It looked like the garden planting was up to Maggie and me. I was relieved she was an experienced gardener, as I had never thought much about how it was done. I was willing to follow instructions. She found the old string marker, and decided it would do for another year. Each end of a long piece of binder twine, the length of the garden, was tied to a sharp stick. It was simple then to push the stick into the soft dirt at one end, and take the other stick to the far end, and line up the string as straight as possible, before sticking it into the dirt. With a hoe, Maggie made a trench along the string. The soil was still moist from the spring melt, and we read the directions on each seed package to find out how deep to plant each variety of vegetables. Maggie told me I could plant my California poppies wherever I chose. I planted them on the edge of the garden, so they would show up when anyone drove in the yard. It was fiddly work to plant the garden. Some seeds were so tiny, you couldn't see them once they were dropped in the row. Corn and beet seeds were easy to see and to place the correct distance apart.

The night before planting, Maggie hauled a pail of old potatoes from the cellar, and showed me how to cut them up, making sure there was an "eye" in each piece. I don't know why she called it an eye. I would have called it a sprout. The potato planting was up to the boys. Dad sent Roy to the potato patch and told him to dig holes a foot apart with the spade. Nick and Will dropped one or two potato sprouts into each hole. They covered each one up and stepped on it to make sure it was well planted. Mac thought he was helping, but he was a bit of a nuisance, and the boys kept telling him to get out of the way. It wasn't long until he decided to come and bother Maggie and me instead.

The field day was an exciting time for my brothers and me, because we could run fast. Mom used to say we could run like the wind. As Roy was working with Dad, it was Will who took on being our coach after school. We found the year before that if we practiced a lot at home, we could bring home the ribbons at the actual Field Day. We rigged up a pole that would do for high jump practice, and also a board dug into the ground that our toe could not go over in long jump. We practiced every living minute that we could. And when the long-awaited Field Day arrived, we did take home the red ribbons. You bet we did! All three of us. Maggie came to the school that day and watched our events. She was mostly busy chasing after Mac, but she was there, I guess, to support us. She had seen us practicing every night at home. I noticed she was chatting with the other parents. Amazing how that woman could talk when she wanted to! She even found a job to do, helping Mrs. Fiske hold the rope at the finish line for the little kids' sack races.

Two of Maggie's hens were out in the barnyard the next day. We had never seen them outside, because they had been faithfully sitting on their nests, out of sight for almost three weeks. They stood out from our bulkier, white, Plymouth Rock chickens. These hens were small and brown, and looked like the Little Red Hen in the storybooks. The mother hens each had a cluster of little chicks. We tried to get a count on them, but they were too fast for us, racing around like little windup toys. By the end of the week, the remaining two hens had also hatched out their chicks. One had a lone chick. She must have had bad luck with the eggs going bad, or getting broken. A little fluff ball like that coming out of an egg was nothing short of a miracle. Who wouldn't love living on the farm, especially in the springtime? I heard Nick ask Maggie if he could have that one little chick for his very own, the one that was alone with his mother. She kind of laughed and said, "Sure, if you want to."

A pair of magpies were building their bushy nest in a tall tree, way too close to the house. The twigs and sticks poking out every which way made it look huge. I mentioned to Will that the little magpies would be so cute, black and white like the parents.

He said, "But what they do isn't so cute! They're the worst birds ever!" Dumb me! I didn't know they were after the baby chicks and the eggs, which explains their setting up housekeeping right beside the chicken house.

Will explained, "That's why Dad usually shoots them." Sure enough, when Dad heard the baby chicks had hatched, he said the magpies had to go. He told the kids to get in the house. He took the shotgun and blasted that big nest to smithereens. He told the boys to keep an eye on the magpies, and if they came back, he would send them to kingdom come.

He also had a hate on for the little red squirrel who was nesting in the granary and making a mess of the oats there. He told Roy to take out the .22 and pick him off. So, we learned we were to value some animals and hate others. This was hard on Nick, because he loved them all.

That summer we added another to the hate list. One evening after supper when Maggie locked the chickens in the henhouse, she came back in and asked if anyone had seen Skipper. We had been playing Anti-I-Over, tossing the ball over the granary. Usually Skipper would have been chasing after us, trying to beat us to the ball, but not one of us remembered seeing him. We were positive he wouldn't go on the road, as Dad had trained him not to go there. Too many first-class farm dogs had been hit on the road by a passing vehicle.

As night came on, and we were almost ready for bed, Dad suggested we all go out and hunt for the dog. He figured Skipper was likely to come if we called him, or if Nick whistled, as we were nicer to him than Dad was. So out we went. Dad lit two lanterns. He gave one to Maggie, and he carried the other. Will swung Mac up on his shoulders, as, of course he wouldn't be able to keep up. As we walked in two small groups, Roy grabbed Nicky and said, "You can ride piggyback, and watch for him better from up there." There we were: Dad, Maggie and us kids, the older boys carrying their little brothers, all searching for the family dog. If that wasn't a cozy family scene, I didn't know what was!

Without discussing where we should look, we all headed towards the pasture. We couldn't see much in the dark, and the lanterns provided a very small circle of light around us. We heard the cowbell every once in a while, when the lead cow back in the barnyard moved around. Dad stopped and held up his hand. All was quiet. Then, we heard it. It was an unmistakable whimpering sound that had to be Skipper. We called him, and the sounds coming out of the bush were louder. Skipper was in there, somewhere inside the bush. We all saw him at the same time, as Dad held the lantern above the dog. He was lying on the grass, dragging his paw over his face, and crying like a baby once he saw us.

We were all talking at once. "What's wrong? What happened?" Dad held the lantern close to Skipper's face.

"He messed with a porcupine, that's what happened," Dad announced. We coaxed the dog to come with us, and he did reluctantly, but probably he sensed we could help him. When we got back to the house, we got Skipper inside. Dad got the needle-nosed pliers from his toolbox, and muttered, "I don't have time for this."

Roy and Will looked at me. "We'll take care of it," Will said. Dad blew out the lanterns and hung them in the porch. Maggie carried Mac upstairs to bed, and they left the job to us. Nick was close to falling asleep, but he was the one who could calm Skipper, so we kept him up. He wouldn't have gone to bed willingly, anyway. Dad left some iodine and Watkin's salve on the table.

Skipper seemed to know we were his best hope. There were a lot of quills sticking into his face, but it didn't look like he had any in his mouth. Roy had heard of dogs trying to bite a porky, and that could be lethal. There we were, all down on the floor holding different parts of our dog, steadying him, quieting him as much as we could. One by one, Roy gripped the quills with the pliers as close to the skin as possible and quickly pulled it straight out. The quills were barbed on the end that pierced the skin, so it must have hurt a lot. Our dog was brave, and so were we. If we left any quills, they would go deeper and cause serious problems, so we took care to get them all out. When we had done all we could, Will poured iodine on the puffy red wounds, and Roy smeared Watkin's salve over top. Skipper was exhausted, and so was Nick. We left Nicky lying by the dog, and I covered them both with a blanket. As my cot was nearby I could keep an eye on them throughout the night. We were proud that we had saved our dog.

The next day Dad, told Roy to take the gun and do away with the porcupine.

"It wasn't his fault," Nick protested.

"Next time, it will be one of the horses," Dad said, "and we can't afford that."

We had recently heard the Grade Twos read aloud the story of "Porky and the Salt", in their *More Streets and Roads* reader. The details were fresh in our minds. In the story, the porcupine outsmarted the fox and gave him a face full of quills. We had taken the porky's side when we read the story, but now, we weren't so sure. Roy shot him the next afternoon. It was up in a tree, gnawing on bark, with his long, orange teeth. He fell like a stone, and Roy and Will buried him, so the quills could never cause trouble again.

Not long after that, we smelled skunk in the yard. Dad told Roy he would give him five bucks if he could find it and shoot it. I thought about the skunk, and its babies somewhere in the woods. Of course, I didn't want our eggs or chickens to be taken by the skunk, but it seemed like no wild animal was safe at the Cleaver farm. I had recently read aloud the Thornton W. Burgess book called *The Adventures of Jimmy Skunk*.

Nick must have been having the same thoughts as I was. "Why do you kill everything?" Nick asked Dad.

Dad shook his head, and said, "If they stay away from here and mind their own business, I'll leave them be. If they interfere with my farm, they're goners!"

One of the positives of attending a one-room school was that we got to hear the lessons for every grade. By the time students finished Grade 8 and left the school, we had heard every story in every reader in every grade. Nicky enjoyed getting in on all the fascinating stories. He especially liked the ones about animals and birds.

The Grade 6 reader had a poem, called "An Indian Arrowhead". Nick, listening in as always, was round-eyed and awestruck. He put up his hand. "Do you think we could we ever find an arrowhead around here?"

Miss Locken said, "I don't know. Class, does anyone know if arrowheads have ever been seen around here?"

Archie Bell raised his hand. "Sure they have! We've found quite a few on our land."

We asked Dad about it when we got home, and he said he had seen one in our north field after a windy day, when the sand was blown off. "That was about a year ago. There it was, a perfect arrowhead with all the little chips on the sides."

Nick was beside himself. "Where is it now, Dad, where is it?"

"I dunno, probably lost it."

Nicky begged to be taken to the north field. We promised we would take him after the next windy day. It was a sure thing he wouldn't have to wait long, as the wind never gave up, gusting every day, till it gave me a headache.

For the rest of the summer, we spent time looking for arrowheads. We found a couple of impressive, whole ones and once we had an idea of what we were looking for, we caught sight of numerous, broken pieces. These were treasures for Nick and he kept them all in a little jar by Dad's tobacco can, on the top of the warming oven.

LAST DAY OF GRADE 5

June 1956

Maggie took off before we left for school, waving to us as she turned Queenie out the lane. She had loaded the buggy early, piling up the four crates that her mom had used to transport the clucky hens. Little Mac was perched on the front seat beside her. She was driving the buggy to her mom's, which meant we were walking to school. We didn't mind. It was a mile and a half, and it was the last day. My second favorite flowers, the brown-eyed susans, and some wild daisies, waved in the breeze on the sides of the road.

To top off a memorable last day of school, the teacher had a surprise for us. She let us out early! She made a little speech, telling us that she had enjoyed her year at our school, and promised she would be back in the fall.

Living in the little teacherage in the schoolyard was probably lonely for her, but I thought she was lucky. I had seen the inside of it one time when some of us girls went there at noon hour to tell her she was wanted on the phone. The teacherage was neat as a pin, and it smelled like Miss Locken's perfume. White curtains let in the sunshine, and pink geraniums bloomed on the window sill. It was a tiny home, with a curtained-off bedroom, a table, cupboard, stove, and a dark green rocking chair. Attached to the wall was a wooden box. It had a large label stuck to the end, picturing yellow pears and the words, "Southern Okanogan, packed and shipped from Oliver, BC." The fruit box had been transformed into a bookcase, to display our teacher's favorite books.

I imagined what it would be like to have a little house like that of my own. One thing for sure, I would have a white cat to keep me company on long winter nights, and I would read lots of books.

Miss Locken wished us all good luck, and a happy summer holiday. Then she called us up to her desk, one by one, to receive our report cards.

"Dorothy." When she called my name, she smiled at me, which I felt was promising. I couldn't resist taking a peek at my report card even before I returned to my desk. Whoa! All "S's"; no "N's" for "Needs Improvement". I finally was doing all "Satisfactory" work! It was Liz who got me trying harder at school. Every Friday while she lived with us, I got 100% on spelling dictation, because she made sure I practiced the list of words at home. And with Will's help I did better in arithmetic. He was a whiz at it, and I was not.

The report card put me in an even better mood. Miss Locken told us we were free to go when we finishing cleaning out our desks. She also said we were welcome to take home any of the school work that we wanted to keep. I saw Will and Roy empty their desks, and throw every last paper in the wastebasket. It was not surprising, as all they wanted to do was to go out to the barn for a smoke with the boys before starting the walk home.

Nick was looking at some of the artwork on his desk, and I could tell he wanted to keep it. I told him, "We are taking all of those home!" He thought I was kidding, until I told him I had already chosen the perfect place to show them off. He grinned from ear to ear, showing that missing front tooth. He handed me his report card with a puzzled look, as if he didn't know what it meant. I grabbed it and turned it over to the back.

"Nickolas Cleaver promoted from Grade 1 to Grade 2, June 28, 1956."

"Way to go, Nicky, you passed into Grade 2, and I'm in Grade 6. Mom would be so proud of us!"

I looked through my desk. All I wanted to keep was the salt and flour map of Canada that Miss Locken had helped me with. Our school had done very well in our entry for prizes in the 1955 Golden Jubilee competition. Saskatchewan celebrated 50 years since it became a province, and had offered a separate contest to all the one-room schools. The teacher submitted a package that included students' poems, artwork, crafts, and my special map of Canada, featuring our province and its resources. Miss Locken made sure she got our school entry in before the deadline, the end of 1955. We had worked hard on our projects, spending some entire Friday afternoons, instead of doing regular school work. The prize we won was a box of brand-new books for our school, some for each grade. As we didn't have books at home, this was like a personal gift to all of us. Every entry had been safely returned. My map was still displayed on the school wall, and even though this was the last day of school, I didn't think I should ask Miss Locken if I could take it home. The judges had written 100% in bright red in the top corner.

I raced to the door with Nick and the others. We all were yelling "goodbye" which was silly, because as soon as we got outside, we decided to stay awhile and eat our lunch together out by the maple trees as we always did. Maybe we were saying goodbye to the school year.

Nick joined Will and Roy, and I could see them far ahead of me which was exactly what I wanted. As I was about to go out of the schoolyard gate, I heard Miss Locken calling, "Dorothy, come back!" There she was on the steps of the school, holding my map.

"You almost forgot this, and what a shame that would be! I'm glad I caught you." I ran back and took it gratefully. I had painted the tips of the mountains white, and I touched my finger to the tallest one. I dreamed of seeing those snow-capped peaks one day.

Miss Locken had told us in class, "You have to see the Rocky Mountains to believe them. They're gigantic! You can't imagine anything that enormous! And they make you feel so small—like an ant!" I think her favorite part of teaching was describing the ocean and mountains and the places she had traveled. I looked at my map from "sea to sea". Someday I would be like Miss Locken and see it all!

I walked a short distance and then stepped off the road to sit on a grassy spot by the fence. This was my time to think back over the school year - my Grade 5 - the good, the bad, and the crazy! Flies were buzzing around some purple clover by my feet. A yellow and black butterfly sailed past me, barely out of my reach.

I could still see the school, with the barn behind it, and the teacherage to the side. It was a busy yard during the school year, but today the door would be locked, and there would be no one coming or going all summer. Probably not long before school started up again in the fall, Bud Turner would bring his tractor and mower to cut the grass. "Briar Rose School #221" was painted in black letters on a sign over the door. I never once said I hated school, like I heard some students say, because I loved to be there. School was like a second home for me, probably because I'd always had kind and caring teachers.

It was a whole year now since Mom left us. I thought over the line of housekeepers we had endured before Dad married Maggie. Our first live-in was miserable Aunt Min. She was useless. Then it was Mrs. Wheeler. Although Mrs. Wheeler worked hard to keep things going at our house, we were too much for her, and she quickly moved on.

When we started school the last of August, Mrs. Wheeler left us. We struggled on our own for part of September, till Nick got sick. That was a significant turning point, when Mrs. Carson, the angel nurse, gave us seven never-to-be-forgotten days. Then Dad hired Liz, and I don't know what would have happened to me if she had not come. She wasn't with us very long, but in the three and a half months she lasted, she was the one who made me feel life was worth living. That is the one thing I could thank Dad for. And then, there was Maggie.

This last day of school was a perfect June morning. I could hear birds twittering, and a gopher whistle as he stood on his hind legs at the opening of his little burrow. I couldn't resist studying my prized map again. All students in Grade 5 made salt and flour maps, but the thin surface had cracked on most of them. Mine was still in good shape. Liz had helped me mix the salt, flour, and water perfectly. I painted the different areas with tempera paint. The bumpy ridges that represented the mountains were a deep blue. The provinces were various colors. I sprinkled salt on a thin line of glue around the borders of Saskatchewan, which made it sparkle and stand out from the other provinces. My map was truly exceptional, and deserving of that red 100%.

Liz had also helped me glue grains of wheat on the wheat-land areas, and we added bits of coal that I picked out of our coal bin to show where the coal mines were located. I had added tiny drawings of orange fish on the coasts, and pictures of cows and horses on cattle country.

Miss Locken told us where she thought our school was located on our maps, close to the middle of the prairie. I marked a little black dot with my pencil on the spot she had selected.

Now as I stared at the spot, I said out loud, "So, that's me...a dot on the prairie!"

I had learned a few lessons during my Grade 5 school year. The number one lesson was right there, staring back at me. Yes, I am only a dot on the wide Canadian prairie, a tiny unimportant speck. But over this past school year, I learned I meant a lot to little Mac and Nick, and I think to Liz, and maybe to others. People might not think much of me or my family, but I remembered the Christmas concert when there were a lot of comments - nice comments - about the Cleaver kids. I held on to that!

It's not about looks either. I had wished since Grade 1 that I was nice-looking like Adele Garnet. I remembered the day Liz cut my hair. I was no better that day with my cute hair-do than I was the day before when my too-long bangs nearly covered my eyes.

So that was the number one lesson I learned in Grade 5. Silly as it sounded, I'm a dot on the prairie, simple as that! I have a purpose and I'm no better and no worse than anyone else. I felt like a wise, old owl. I would watch for life lessons in the summer ahead. As I walked towards home, I thought about where I would store my special map. I knew it would go into Mom's special blue trunk.

KNOCK ME DOWN
WITH A FEATHER!

A couple of days later, I discovered Maggie was hiding a whopping secret. Now that school was out and summer holidays were ours to enjoy, I was thinking the wild strawberries might be ready. I headed down the curvy cow path to the east pasture where the berries had been plentiful last year at this time. I took a cup along in case.

Sure enough, I spied some ripe ones right away in a flat, sandy spot where the sun could get at them. I popped a couple in my mouth. They were small but oh, they were juicy. There is nothing that comes close to the taste of ripe wild strawberries! In two seconds, I was on my knees where I could see lots more berries from down there. The ants had got to some of them before I did, but my cup was filling up fast. I heard the distinctive call of a meadowlark.

"I see teacher's petticoat," it sang. The bird was close by on the fence post, its black V standing out on its bright yellow breast. There it was again. "I see teacher's petticoat!" I didn't mind the bees humming beside me. Summer holidays! I remembered how much I loved the easy days of summer. No school, no cold weather, and hopefully, fewer chores. I was a fast berry picker, and the cup was soon filled up to the top. As I stood up, I glanced again at the meadowlark's fence post. The bird was gone, but what I saw nearly made me drop my cup. Of all the sights I had not expected, who should be standing there, but Maggie! She hadn't seen me and was staring out towards the fence that ran along the roadside.

The breeze had picked up a bit. Her wild, red hair was flying around her face, and her loose shirt for the moment was pressed against her middle.

Oh. My. Golly. I stared at her. Well, actually I stared at her belly. Liz had told me a lot of things. She said it was the "birds and bees talk". Maggie heard me just then. I guess I surprised her. She snapped at me, "What are you doing here?" She acted like I had no business being in our own pasture.

"Picking strawberries. What are *you* doing here?"

Her eyes were nearly shut, maybe it was the sun. I know red-haired people have trouble with the sun. Maybe that's why her eyes were almost slits as she looked at me.

"Trying to get away from all of you."

Of course, no one else was there to hear me, and I was feeling bold and sassy. "That's a mean thing to say, Maggie."

She must have felt bold and sassy, too, because she spoke back. "I hate you, Dot. I hate all of you."

I gave her both barrels. "Well, that's no surprise. Tell me something I don't know. Of course, you hate us! You won't talk to us, and you treat us like we're poison." That shut her up. She pursed her lips and held them together like she wanted to say something else, but wouldn't.

"Do you hate the boys, too, or only me?"

"I said all of you." That's when I saw tears falling down the freckles on the side of her face that I could see. My heart melted a little - I never was okay with tears. I didn't cry very often myself. I had the idea that if I ever got sad enough to cry, I wouldn't be able to stop. She was still gazing at the road. I decided to be a little bit nice, and it's true, I was curious.

"So when are you going to have your baby?" She was breathing hard, I think to keep from crying. When I said "baby", her hand went straight to her belly. She probably wondered how I knew.

I could hardly hear her answer, "I guess about October or November."

I couldn't help it. I was thinking about the birds and the bees talk. "Do you hate my Dad, too?" She wouldn't look at me, but she answered much louder this time.

"I didn't say that."

I started for the house. I wanted her to say, "Stop, Dot, I didn't mean it. I don't hate you." But she had said it, and she must have meant it. I decided as I raced home, "Okay, fine, I'll hate her right back!"

At the house I emptied my cup. The berries had gone all soft and were sticking together, but Nicky and Little Mac grabbed some even before I spread them out on a plate. Roy and Will each ate a handful, stems and all. That was the end of them.

"I know something you don't know," I said, rolling my eyes to get them wondering.

Roy grinned. "And Will and I know something you don't!"

"Okay, what?" Their news would be nothing compared to mine!

"Oh, it's not earth-shaking. Dad's mad. He found out me and Will were smokin' his tobacco."

"What did he say?"

Will grinned. "He didn't say nothin', but he glared at us. He'll find a better hiding place for his outside stash, that's all."

I was disgusted with my brothers. "How can you guys stand to smoke? It's awful and it stinks!"

Roy shrugged his shoulders, "Aw, we're just trying to make him mad!"

Our family sure wasn't all love and kisses. The boys were always trying to get Dad's goat, and less than half an hour ago, Maggie, our so-called stepmother said she hated us all. Roy and Will each took a drink from the dipper that floated in the water pail. As they headed outside, Roy, stopped. "And what's your stupendous news, Dot?"

I couldn't wait any longer, so I burst out with it, "Maggie's gonna have a baby!"

Will's eyebrows shot straight up, and Roy slowly shook his head before they went out the door. I had a lot of thinking to do. Which was worse? Maggie admitting she hated us, or that she was having a baby? Why on earth did Dad marry her? Did he think she would be a mom to us, or was he looking for a free housekeeper?

I didn't have long to think about it, because I heard Dad yelling at the boys in the yard. Will shouted, "We're getting a drink!" Will could get away with yelling back, but never Roy! Of course Dad was giving them heck for being in the house instead of working.

I decided to go upstairs in case I was next in line to get yelled at, and I took the broom to prove that I was doing something, in case he checked on me. Maggie wasn't back yet, probably still feeling sorry for herself in the strawberry patch. I swept the boys' bedroom, even way back under the beds. There were round balls of dirt under there and some socks. I pulled the blankets up and smoothed them out on each bed. Nick's pictures that he brought from the school were piled on the dresser. I put them by the door, so I would remember to keep my promise of displaying them.

The other bedroom door was slightly open. Maggie usually made up that bed, but not today. I walked in, thinking to sweep under their bed, too, and as soon as I stepped inside, I thought of the past months, sharing this same room with the various ladies who had been in our life in the past year—Aunt Hazel, old Aunt Min, Mrs. Wheeler, and Liz. I also remembered the day my Mom died and the pile of sheets that were in the corner. I quickly backed out of the room.

When Maggie came back to the house, she acted like nothing had happened. In my book, you don't tell somebody you hate them and then expect everything to be the same as before. Every time I looked at her, I thought first of her little potbelly, and second, I remembered how she said, "I hate all of you." It was hard to let it go.

After supper, Will motioned to me to follow him outside. He didn't say anything as he pointed to the plant Mom and I had relocated to the shade of the house. I dropped to my knees when I saw the tender heart-shaped leaves framing a bunch of purple violets. I studied the tiny faces of those flowers, and my heart ached. At that moment, I didn't care one bit that Maggie hated me, because the violets were proof that my Mom still loved me.

DREAMS DO COME TRUE

Maggie didn't like to hear me talk about Liz. "You go on and on about her as if she's your long-lost fairy godmother! Every day, all day long."

It was true. I did talk about her a lot. Liz was the best part of this last year since Mom died. "I'll talk about her if I want to, Maggie. I don't even know where she went."

Maggie frowned. "You don't know where she is?" I shook my head.

"Well, I do. She's in the mental hospital - probably not far from where your aunt lives."

I was stunned. I couldn't believe my ears. Why didn't anybody tell me? She lived that close? Aunt Hazel lived in Stillwater, thirty miles from our farm. And what did Maggie know about Liz? Did Dad tell her?

"Well, if you want to see her that bad, I'll take you there myself!" I knew Maggie was bragging, and I didn't believe her for a minute. She couldn't take me anywhere. The only place she had gone since the day she arrived was to town with Dad to get groceries, when we were at school. Oh yeah, she did go to her mom's a couple of times with the horse and buggy.

Maggie loved knowing something I didn't, so she warmed up to telling me about the hospital. She had seen a picture of it on a postcard. It was a huge red brick building with tall chimneys, and there were trees and gardens all around it. She explained that her aunt had lived there for a few months, and she was sure people could go visit the patients there.

It took "some doing" for both Maggie and I, but we had success, and my dream of visiting Liz came true. At Maggie's suggestion,

I wrote a letter to my Aunt Hazel in the city. I told her I was trying to get a ride for Dad's new wife and me to come and visit for a day. I still resented my aunt being so secretive after Mom died, even when she was staying with us, back at the beginning. I wish we had begged her to tell us how and why it happened. We should have made her tell us. It was like there was an elephant in the room. We were all thinking about it night and day, but she didn't breathe a word, and we were afraid to ask. Maybe we were afraid to know. So, in my letter, I decided to hold nothing back. No secrets from me! I even told her about Maggie being pregnant. I told her, too, that I wanted to find Liz.

Maggie produced an envelope and a stamp. Maggie had a friend from school that she wrote to every week. I hadn't noticed any of her mail lying around, but that would be because I didn't take much interest in Maggie's personal life. I had never written a letter before, except for a practice one at school. Maggie found out the address, and I didn't have to wait long for a reply. Aunt Hazel wrote back immediately.

"Dear Dorothy,

You are welcome to come any Saturday or Sunday. I went to the Provincial Hospital and they confirmed Liz is still a patient there and it is possible for you to visit her.

I will get a few things together for you kids. I have been feeling guilty for not doing that sooner. My house address is 182 Railway Avenue. I hope you can get a ride.

As ever, Aunt Hazel"

The news about Liz made me ecstatic. It was the greatest news ever! Maggie was quite proud of herself for getting that part settled. She arranged the ride, too, as easy as pie.

Roy mentioned on a Friday morning that the saskatoons on the north road were thick, and ready to be picked. Maggie and I called Nick and Mac and told them to put on their shoes because we were going to pick berries. Maggie and I each buckled a belt around our waists to hold a pail. That way, we could hold a branch steady with one hand, and strip off the berries with the other. I laughed at Maggie as she tried to fasten the belt above the baby bulge, and then under it, where it finally fit. We gave the boys smaller containers and the four of us walked down the road, where the saskatoon bushes were purple with fruit.

On the shady side of the saskatoon bushes, I discovered three flaming orange tiger lilies. I quickly called Nick, and he knelt down on the ground beside them. I explained what Miss Locken had told us - that they are Saskatchewan's special flower, properly called the Western Lily, and we weren't allowed to pick them. They were so striking and so vibrant, that we looked at them for a long time.

The gophers were having a heyday on the road. They had burrowed on the edges, in the ditches, and some of their holes were on the main road. They were cheeky, waiting till we were almost beside them, before shaking their tails and vanishing into the ground. Of course, we hated gophers as much as rats and mice. They did a lot of damage to the crops. Most kids, especially the boys, knew how to drown them out of their holes by pouring water into each entrance, and whacking them on the head with a stick when they emerged.

Soon after we arrived at the berry patch, we heard a vehicle approaching and quickly recognized Mrs. Fiske at the wheel. Maggie stood close to the edge of the road and got a face full of dust as the truck came to a stop. Mrs. Fiske commented on how plentiful the saskatoons were, and said it was ambitious of us to get out and pick them. Very quickly, Maggie saw her chance and asked, "Say, are you planning to go to the city sometime this summer?"

Mrs. Fiske got excited. "Yes! As a matter of fact, we're going tomorrow!" How perfect was that! Tomorrow was Saturday and my aunt had said to come on a weekend! In a few minutes it was all set. Fiskes would pick us up at eight in the morning. As we trooped back to the house with our buckets overflowing, I asked Maggie if she would ask Dad.

She grinned at me and said, "No, I won't ask, but I'll tell him!"

The next morning, Dad took his wallet out of his jacket in the closet and pulled out a blue five-dollar bill. He handed it to Maggie, looking at the money and not at her, like he was sad to see it go.

Maggie raised her eyebrows. "Can I get you something?"

"Nothing I need," he said as the screen door shut behind him. The boys were round-eyed. Five bucks! Lucky her. None of us had ever had any money of our own. Maggie was suddenly in a festive mood.

"Okay, I'm buying candy!"

"And popcorn?" asked Nicky.

"You bet, popcorn, too!" I wondered if she would, or if she'd spend it on herself.

I was so glad we'd brought jackets. The sun was already hot but once we got riding in the back of Fiske's truck, the speed created a chilly wind. We cuddled down on the floor with our backs against the cab, but the wind still whipped our hair like crazy. Fence posts, telephone poles, and even the willows in the ditches streaked past us. It seemed like we were going way faster than we ever had in the back of Dad's truck. There was a wooden egg crate beside me and a cream can with "Fred Fiske" painted on it. I guessed we would be dropping off the cream at the city creamery. That would be interesting. We had two cream cans at home, both marked "R. Cleaver". About every five or six days Dad dropped off a full can at the train station in town, and in a few days, the payment came in the mail. I asked Mom one time how much the cheque was for and she said it depended on the "test". If the cream was to their liking, we got more money, but sometimes the test was poor, if the cows happened to eat some stinkweed and the taste got into the cream. There was another way to improve the test and that was to adjust the cream screw in the separator. Mom said there was a person called the "taster" at the creamery. What a horrible job to taste cream all day!

Another horrible job was washing the cream separator at home, twice a day. Dad showed Will and me how to do it properly when we were first by ourselves. The separator was an amazing invention that separated the cream from the skim milk. There were 12 discs to wash, and then rinse with boiling water from the tea kettle. The way it worked was the whole milk was poured into the round metal bowl at the top. The milk then passed through the machine, and moved through the holes in those discs. Somehow that process magically sent the cream out one spout to go into the cream can for sale at the creamery. The skimmed milk poured out the second spout to feed kids and cats and pigs! If anyone of us kids would become an inventor, I would bet on Roy. He had tried to explain to us how the separator worked, but we didn't get it.

The ride in the truck went fast, as my mind was whirling around, thinking about eggs and cream tasters, all the while trying not to count too much on seeing Liz in case it didn't turn out.

Mr. Fiske seemed to know his way around the city, and drove us directly to my aunt's house. Mrs. Fiske told us that she was friends with my aunt and she had known my Mom, too. They had gone to school together in the same grade, and Aunt Hazel was one grade behind them.

Fiskes dropped us off, and were gone with a wave out the truck window. Mrs. Fiske called cheerfully, "See you girls at five!"

Aunt Hazel had lunch ready for us --ham and cheese in buns, beet pickles, and yummy potato salad. One of my biggest goals in life was to learn was how to make delicious food. I would always remember Liz's good cooking, and I still had the recipes she wrote out for me. As if reading my mind about Liz, my aunt said she would drop us off at the hospital in a little while. After lunch, Maggie helped Aunt Hazel with the dishes. Finally, Maggie was acting like an adult for a change, and I was the kid! My aunt told me I could play with their orange mother cat in the back yard. I didn't care much for the cat, but I pumped myself up on the rope swing. I got myself up so high, I could see into the neighboring yards. I wondered what it would be like to live in town. I wished we had a swing. Aunt Hazel's kids were about the age of Roy, so the swing wasn't in use. I wished I could transplant it into our yard for Nick and Mac! She said her boys were away for the weekend on a Boy Scout camping trip with their dad. Even though they were our cousins, we didn't know them very well. I thought of Will and Roy working hard out in the hayfield, sweating and dirty. Wouldn't they love a Boy Scout camp! Well, those things weren't for us Cleavers.

Maggie lied at the desk-- outright lied -- to the nurse. She said we were Liz Parker's nieces, and that seemed to be our ticket in. We followed her white stockings and wide bum down one pale green corridor after another. We turned countless corners. I could never find my way out. Maggie was having an adventure. "I used to visit my other aunt here," she explained, but the nurse who was guiding us paid no attention.

"It's an awful place, Dot, you'll see." The nurse must have heard her, but the circular movement of her backside in front of us never slowed down.

Seconds later, we heard shrieking and crying from a side corridor. I wondered if the woman was okay and if anyone was helping her. Maggie grinned, unconcerned.

"See, I told you. Some wings are locked down. It's enough to curl your hair." I hoped Maggie wouldn't say such things when we finally got to see Liz.

"I'm sure Aunt Liz will be in dandy shape," Maggie assured me, obviously enjoying her play-acting. "She's been in here long enough to be on the right medication. I'm surprised she's still in here."

I wondered if the nurse suspected we weren't related to Liz after all. I gave Maggie a dark look to tone it down.

Finally, a door was opened in front of us where the walls were yellow instead of green. Our brisk nurse kept moving and motioned to us to follow. "Come along, she's over here by the window." Instantly, I recognized the back of Liz's head. Of course, it was her, and my heart skipped a beat. The nurse tapped Liz none too gently on the shoulder, "Your nieces are here!"

The nurse disappeared. It was "sink or swim", "do or die"! What if Liz wasn't Liz anymore?! I remembered the last time I saw her. Maybe she would be doped up on pills and not recognize me.

I stood in front of her and I had trouble turning up the volume. "Liz, it's me, Dot." Crazy tears poured down my cheeks and Liz reached out her long arms. Maggie rolled her eyes, but thankfully she said nothing.

It was the most wonderful day in my memory, or at least for a long, long while. Liz was doing well, she said. As always, she told it all. She said she took pills each day, and could even leave the hospital if she had some relatives to sign her out. That seemed the time to tell her about us being her nieces. Liz laughed long and loud about Maggie's fib!

She told us she'd been worried about us ever since they took her away. Liz was always easy to talk to, and I told her everything I could think of. I told her Dad was married. She raised her eyebrows and asked, "And do you have a wicked stepmother?"

I shook my head and pointed at Maggie's belly. "Nope, not exactly wicked, but she is pregnant."

Liz was genuinely pleased. "Hopefully, your Dad will be happier now. He seemed lost when I was there." Same old Liz, saying something nice about the person who was being criticized. I wonder if she'd think so kindly of him if she knew he called her "Crazy Liz" and said she had gone to the "nut house".

At 3:30, an attractive young lady in a pink and white striped uniform came in and asked Liz if she wanted to go to the tea room.

"Are my nieces welcome?" Liz asked with her extra-large grin.

The girl shook her head, "Sorry, Liz."

Liz called after her, "Thanks anyway Margaret, but I'm staying here with my girls." Dear Liz. Always the cheery sport - well not always, but for sure always when she was well.

I told Liz about our hard times without her, about Maggie coming, and Dad not even telling us he was getting married. I was letting it all out, venting in a safe place. "I hate him now," I said, and I expected Liz would be on my side. I didn't think she would respond the way she did.

"Oh Dot. You can't hate him. He's your Dad and he's the dad of this upcoming baby, too." She pointed at Maggie's round belly when she said it.

For once, someone was listening to me and my troubles. I wanted to tell Liz everything. I felt like I had to get it all out before we had to go. I wished Maggie wasn't sitting there soaking up every word, but it was my chance.

"You know how he treats us."

"I'll say it again, Dot, you can't hate him."

"How can I stop myself, Liz?"

"By deciding not to hate him, that's how. So much of life is in our attitude. Believe me, Honey-girl, I know. I hated my dad, too."

"Was he awful?"

"Yes, he was, definitely. There were lots of reasons to hate him, but it was only hurting me." There were those tears again. Liz was right. It was hurting me.

Liz reached over to me and patted my hand. "Let it go, Dot. Loving is easier than hating."

I could tell Maggie was finding our conversation awkward, and very soon after that, she cheerfully announced it was time to go. She wasn't kidding, as the clock on the wall was creeping up to four o'clock. We had been there for an hour, and my aunt would soon be waiting out in front. I didn't care what Maggie thought of me. I threw my arms around Liz's neck and held on. She was the one to say goodbye. Of course she was. When had Liz ever been short of words?

"Way you go, Honey-girl. Your visit has put a song in my heart."

Maggie smiled at me as if she were looking after a small child.

"Well, bye-bye," she said, obviously glad to be getting out of there. Liz nodded and waved as we left the yellow room and started down the green hallway. Maggie amazed me. She quickly found our way up one hallway and down another, and with a couple of twists and turns, we were back where we started at the front desk. She signed us out in the visitor book, at the same time as my aunt's old brown Plymouth pulled up by the door outside. What a day! I had a song in my heart, too, just like Liz! I hopped in the back seat, and Maggie got in the front beside my aunt, observing the old unwritten rule that the oldest has the privilege of sitting by the driver.

"Dot's bawling," Maggie announced with a glance over her shoulder.

"I am not!" Even as I denied it, the tears kept falling on my already wet blouse.

My aunt looked at me in the rearview mirror. "Tears are okay, Dorothy." I remembered the tide of tears Aunt Hazel couldn`t stop the day her sister died.

Then she looked over at Maggie and said kindly, "Maggie, if you and I are honest, I'll bet we've both shed our share of tears. Life isn't always easy." Maggie didn't protest, and to me her silence was admitting she wasn't as tough as she pretended.

I had a question for my aunt before our day was over, so I spoke up on the way. "Liz says she can get out if someone signs for her. Is that true?" Aunt Hazel wheeled around a corner a little too quickly, and I was glad I was hanging on to the strap hanging above my head. She nodded, and said matter-of-factly, "Yes, that's probably exactly right. But if she doesn't have family to take responsibility for her, she's likely stuck in there for good."

We were all quiet as we pulled up in front of 182 Railway Avenue. "Did Liz seem to be doing okay?" Aunt Hazel asked.

Maggie trotted behind us into the house. Before I could answer, she chirped, "Oh yeah, she loves it there." It was my turn to roll my eyes.

The house was surrounded by trees and was cool inside. How I wished I could live in the city! It was cleaner than the farm. There were flowers by the sidewalk, and a neatly mowed patch of thick, green grass. At home, I hated the milk separator and milk pails that we had to wash in the kitchen and most of all, I despised the chicken poop all over our yard.

My aunt had borrowed some attractive smocks for Maggie to wear during her pregnancy. The women held them up one by one, and I could tell Maggie was pleased. Aunt Hazel cautioned her to be careful of them, and return them after the baby was born. She also came up with a box of baby clothes and little blankets. She gave us a tin pail filled with homemade cookies, and a box of old toys that her kids had long ago outgrown. I peeked in and saw lots of trucks and cars, some farm animals, and an old soccer ball. I thanked her so much and told her the boys would be over the moon.

She put her arm around me as we walked out the door. Maggie was already out there waiting for our ride, and had piled the stuff from my aunt by the sidewalk.

"You're a sweet girl, Dorothy. Study hard at school, and someday your life will be a lot better than it is now." I hung on to her promise even though I didn't know exactly what she meant. I still had an important question for her, but I didn't dare ask it.

Maggie and I climbed back into the truck, which was a little awkward for Maggie, but she didn't seem to think anything of her protruding belly. We hung on tightly to the bags my aunt had so generously sent with us. We got ourselves positioned against the shelter of the truck cab. Mrs. Fiske tapped on the little window above our heads and pointed to us. I wondered if something was wrong but she mouthed the words, "Are you okay?" We were fine, so we nodded and waved back at her. I would always be thankful to them for this memorable day. My aunt's words were ringing in my mind. How could my life be better if I study? Maybe she thought I could one day become a teacher or a nurse. After today, I didn't want to be a nurse, but I should start thinking about what job I could get in my future. Imagine having money of my own! What if someday I became a teacher living in a little teacherage and I could check Liz out of that scary place! But that would never happen. I did decide though, then and there, that with Grade 6 coming up, I would give it all I had.

The trip made Maggie giddy. I think she was proud of herself that she had pulled it off, as she had promised. She was yelling at me, and pointing out various sights as we rode home, until she finally caught on that the noise of Fiskes' truck and the wind in our ears was drowning out everything she tried to say. Instead, she elbowed me every time she saw anything of interest. Finally, she pointed to a car that had broken down on the side of the road. Kids were playing in the ditch. Presumably they had been traveling in the car. Mr. Fiske pulled to a stop after we passed them, and walked back to see if he could help. Soon the truck box was full of the kids and their parents, all squashing in so tight there was no danger of anyone falling out. I hoped Fiskes' truck would hold together until we got home. They appeared to be leaving the car alone on the edge of the road, at least for the time being.

I doubted Maggie had bought the treats she promised, or the popcorn, as I had been with her the whole day. I suspected she still had that five-dollar bill in her hot little hand. The boys would be mad and Nick would be broken-hearted. But that was Maggie - what could you expect! When we decided on the trip to the city, Maggie suggested we both needed a change of scenery. She'd been to the city once before, and I had never been, at least not that I could remember.

We got off at our lane and thanked our generous neighbors for the ride. They continued on with their extra passengers, and we hurried to the house. Once inside, Maggie dumped out a bag of gum and candy and box of Lucky Elephant pink popcorn! Oh wow! She must have given the money to my aunt to shop while we were at the hospital. I saw her put a Cuban Lunch chocolate bar on top of Dad's tobacco can on the stove. How did she know he liked that kind?

The boys dived into the treats. I thought about Liz's words: "Loving is easier than hating." I had been so quick to think the worst of Maggie, yet she had sacrificed her time in the city to make sure I saw Liz, and had, after all, shared her loot with us kids. Not so very long ago in the pasture she said she hated all of us, but it seemed she may have changed her mind.

MORE SECRETS

It was in July that we got the phone, a real phone, like they had at the school. Dad and the boys had to help put in telephone poles from the end of the line at Fiskes' farm to ours. It was a few day's work, but when it was done, we watched in amazement as the telephone man with a leather pouch hanging with tools, came into our house and asked Maggie, "Well, where do you want it? Here or here?"

She chose the spot he pointed to that was closest to the window facing the lane. I thought it was a sensible call, because if someone phoned for Dad we could see if he was in the yard or not.

By that evening, we had a phone attached to the wall, and the telephone book hanging on a hook screwed into the wallboard. Our number was Line 4, ring 1-4. Now that would be a lot of cranking if anyone wanted to give us a call. Dad told us never to take down the receiver unless we were sure it was our number, one long and four shorts. He said listening in to telephone conversations was called "rubbernecking" and it was the same as stealing. The telephone man had tested the phone by calling a few numbers, including the switchboard in town which was operated by his wife. Later, Dad told me to see if I could call the Fiskes. I looked up their number, Line 4, ring 1-1. They were on the same line as we were, so all I had to do was turn the crank for one long ring and then one very short one. I heard a voice at the other end of the line.

"Hello, Colleen Fiske here."

I was tongue-tied. I mumbled, "It's Dot."

"Hello Dot. Oh yes, you've got the phone now."

I was nervous, but I managed to speak. "We're trying out the phone."

"Well, it's working fine! Give us a ring anytime, dear. Bye-bye."

The family had been listening to my feeble effort. Roy paged through the phone book and grinned as he pressed the silencing button on the side, and cranked a long ring. He told me later that's how to call the switchboard.

He surprised us all, acting like he had been using the phone all his life. He told the operator, "Line 5, ring 1-2." She must have put his call through quickly, as after a moment we heard him say, "Hello Louise, this is Hec!"

Early one morning in July, a bay mare pulling a buggy trotted into the yard. It was Maggie's mother, leaning forward on the buggy seat. I could tell it was her by the long red, bushy hair. She had no teeth and I couldn't help but look at her tongue darting in and out of her mouth. Maggie didn't introduce us, but she quickly unloaded some plants from the buggy. There were little lilac trees and a lot of the homestead plant called Maltese Cross. I always wanted to have some of that in our yard because the flowers were such a deep red, and Mrs. Fiske insisted you couldn't kill that plant if you tried. There were clumps of thick dirt sticking to the roots, and I figured if we quickly planted them with a good shot of water, they probably would catch on and grow in our yard. She also brought mint, fragrant and green, that spreads wherever you plant it. So, we were finding out a little about Maggie. She seemed to love plants and gardening - and chickens. Her mom also brought a wooden egg crate full of eggs. She must have quite the chicken ranch over there.

I watched Maggie and her mother. They hardly spoke to each other. Maggie lifted a box that looked quite heavy out of the back of the buggy. If I'd known what was in it, I would have rushed to help her carry it. Her mom didn't even say goodbye or wave. She whacked the lines a couple of times on the horse's rump, and hurried out the lane.

About ten minutes later, Mrs. Fiske steered their blue truck into our yard and parked near our summer kitchen, where we were shelling peas in the shade. She carried an armful of freshly cut rhubarb.

"I thought you girls might like to make a pie." As she said it, she raised her eyebrows as if asking if we actually could manage to make a pie. She always referred to us as "girls". She also brought a chocolate cake that didn't last past noon.

We thanked Mrs. Fiske so much for the rhubarb and the cake, and she went on her way. I had noticed she was wearing the same flowered dress she wore to the school picnic back in June, but it looked a lot shorter on her now. I asked Maggie if she thought maybe Mrs. Fiske was pregnant.

"Nope. She's just getting fat," Maggie declared. "She told me at the picnic that she can't have any kids. That's why she likes Mac so much." Maggie figured she was an expert on everything. If she said it, then I was expected to believe it was the gospel truth.

Our talk of Mrs. Fiske possibly being pregnant must have reminded Maggie of her situation. She said out of the blue,

"The baby's started kicking a lot." Oh, so apparently, she knew all about this, too! An expert on pregnancy.

"How do you know it's the baby? Maybe it's something you ate and you're …"

Maggie quickly interrupted me. "Oh, I know what it feels like, don`t worry."

I snapped back at her, "I'm not worrying - it's your baby! I just wondered how you know so much about it."

The day was hot. Beads of sweat were standing out on Maggie's forehead and she looked exhausted. She wore a baggy old shirt. I wished she would wear one of the smocks Aunt Hazel had loaned her, but she told me before that she was saving them "for good."

Maggie stared past me, down the road where her mother had disappeared in a cloud of buggy dust a half-hour before.

"I do know what it's like, because I had a baby two years ago. So don't tell me I don't know!"

I was flabbergasted. I felt my forehead pucker in amazement.

"You had a baby! How come?"

"Don't be stupid, Dot. Don't say how come."

"Well, where is it?"

Maggie closed her eyes, obviously remembering. She wiped the sweat off her face with the long sleeve of her shirt.

"The baby was taken away from me. My mother made arrangements to adopt it out."

"Was it a girl or a boy?"

"Boy."

I had another question, but this time I was nicer. "Would you like this baby to be a girl?"

"Yeah."

It finally registered in my little pea brain that the baby Maggie was growing inside her could be the sister I'd always wanted. I wondered, as I had before, how Maggie felt about my dad. I remembered that unforgettable day in the strawberry patch when she said she hated all of us, but even though she was off the wall that day, she wouldn't admit to hating Dad.

I asked her why she married a man with five kids. I thought it was a fair question, but I didn't expect an answer. Her reply was something I'll never forget. "If you have a baby before you're married, everything changes. You don't have the same choices after that."

I felt braver. "So, how did you meet Dad, anyway?"

Maggie had a little smirk on her face.

"I'll never tell." I knew Dad would never tell either, so they could keep their little secret.

SAVING THE GARDEN

J uly was awful. Early mornings were bright and fresh, but by noon the hot, dry wind picked up a bit and then blew and blew all afternoon. It flung dust in our hair and dirt in our eyes. The annoying wind and the boiling sun joined forces to wring the fun out of the summer holidays.

I complained to Maggie. "Don't you despise this wind?"

She looked confused. "No, why would I?"

"Because it just won't stop!"

Maggie shrugged her shoulders and looked at me strangely. "You can't change the wind, Dot!"

The day after our trip to the city, the weather got even hotter, burning hot, and we simply couldn't cool off. Finally, I thought of the cellar. I got Roy to lift the trap door in the kitchen floor and turn on the light. Nick and little Mac and I went down the steps after Roy promised we wouldn't be forgotten down there. The boys and I played Twenty Questions for a while. It was a welcome escape from the heat outside and upstairs. The cool cellar wasn't the most pleasant place though, because it smelled musty. The last of the stored potatoes and carrots were at the bottom of the bin, and the onions were withered and dry, most of them flat and useless as they had hung in bunches there all winter. The shelves where sealers of fruit and vegetables had been were almost bare. They were dusty, and needed a good wipe down. Only jars of beet pickles and canned rhubarb were left. I had a feeling we were not alone, as there were probably mice down there who had found themselves a winter home.

We should have been using new garden produce by now, but the bedraggled plants were as hot and thirsty as we were. Dad filled two barrels with water from the well, and hauled them on the stoneboat to the east end of the vegetable rows. He and Roy went mowing hay, while the rest of us were left with instructions to water the garden by dipping small pails in the barrels, and pour water on the parched ground. The day was long and hot, and we were cooked by noon. The boys' faces were as red as mine, and Maggie fared no better, with sunburn on her arms and forehead. She made a bunch of peanut butter sandwiches, which we washed down with water, as we sat on the ground in the shade of the house. After a short break, we went back at it. Maggie made extra sandwiches for the hay mowers, and left a plateful on the table, covered with a tea cloth to keep off the flies.

I couldn't help but wish we were back in school. I didn't know summer was going to be like this. Maggie brought a two quart sealer of water outside, and a cup, and told us to drink lots. Each time one of us took a cup of water, we threw the last of it on someone else. It was a relief to get even a tiny bit wet, and Maggie didn't mind when Nick threw a whole cup on her. Finally, the second barrel was empty, and the garden had a skinny, wet track down each row. We may have saved the garden that day. By the next morning some of the plants looked revived, like they wanted to try again.

On the days I disliked Maggie, I said over and over in my head, "She's dumb as a post." And then I'd feel guilty, because she had helped me get to the city to see Liz, and she came up with a smart idea or two that worked. One was how to make wallpaper paste. I told her I had an idea to glue Nick's Grade 1 artwork on the inside of the outhouse walls, and did she know how we could do it?

She said, "Sure, I made gallons of wallpaper paste when Mom and I papered our whole house last year." We watched as she mixed water and flour, along with a little alum from the pickling spices shelf. I asked why it needed the alum, and she said she didn't know, but it's how she made it before. She heated the mixture on the stove, stirred the lumps out of it, and proudly handed me a cup of warm paste. Nick and I were soon spreading it nice and thick on the back of all his drawings and displaying them where every family member could take a long look.

SUMMER KITCHEN

Maggie had another idea that turned out to be superior. That was the summer kitchen. She got the idea when she came across an old cook stove in the shade of the bush, not far from the house. It was rusting to death out there, since we got a better stove a couple of years ago at a neighbor's auction sale. The oven door had the name McLaren on it, but the hinge was broken, so we couldn't get it closed. The old stove had seen better days, but apparently, we were getting it back in service.

"Your dad says we can try cooking on the old stove," Maggie told us. She always said "your dad". I never heard her call him "Robert", which made it feel like he was the dad of us all, even Maggie.

So, she bossed us into helping her make an outdoor kitchen. There wasn't much to it, but we all lent a hand, first raking out the old grass and leaves from around and under the stove. We stuck a brick under one stove leg to level it out. I got a pail of water and a rag to scrub off the worst of the dirt and cobwebs. The boys emptied the ashes, and filled the reservoir with water. The fresh water we poured into it instantly turned a dark red-brown, but Maggie said we needed that rusty water handy, in case the sparks escaped the stove pipe and started a fire.

She and Will cut off the branches of the trees that were too close to the back of the stove. He also helped her attach an old stovepipe that was buried in the dry, dead grass. We banged the soot and rust out of it, and got it hooked on, pointing straight up. Maggie wired a double layer of old window screen across the top to make it safer. We were getting the feel of it.

We could imagine how nice it would be not to always be heating the house by cooking in the kitchen. It would also keep the house cooler for sleeping. The boys said the upstairs was sweltering at night, and downstairs on my cot, it wasn't much better. Will dragged a long table out of the shed near the barn. We scrubbed it with soap, and found a couple of tippy benches that had been discarded behind the shed. So there - we had a kitchen and a dining room! Maggie sent us for kindling and dry sticks from the bush, and we brought armloads of stove wood from the woodpile. It was like setting up a playhouse and I kept thinking Dad would be mad, but that night when we sat down for supper, he admitted it was better than eating in the heat of the house.

Maggie had boiled macaroni on the stove, added a jar of tomatoes, and fried up some ham. She put coffee on to boil. Our supper in the yard proved the battered old stove was working. Of course, we were forever running back and forth to the house to get this and that from the kitchen, but it was worth it. We heated water in the dishpan on the stove for washing dishes later. We were still eating when Mr. Fiske drove in the lane. He took off his sweaty cap and rubbed his arm across his forehead.

"Now there's an idea! I'll tell the missus what the neighbors are up to!"

Before bed, Maggie set the paper, kindling, and wood in the outside stove. She got the coffee pot ready for morning, too. We were up and out there early in the morning, even though the dew was wet and cold on our bare feet. Maggie cooked porridge, while we took turns running to the house for dishes and spoons and brown sugar.

SUMMER DAYS

August 1956

So, with the novelty of our summer kitchen, we were getting through the hot, dry summer. It felt like we were camping in our yard. Nothing like the fancy Boy Scout camp our cousins in the city got to go to, but the Cleavers could make something out of nothing and that made us proud.

Dark clouds rolled in after a sweltering day. The wind began to blow, sudden and strong, and the sky turned dark. It blew an old pail across the barnyard, the chickens headed for the henhouse, and we hurried into the house ourselves. It started with a few fat drops of rain on the windows and then it became hard rain, pelting down and drumming on the roof. Roy and Will were soaking wet in the few minutes it took them to get into the house from the barn. The summer had been so hot and dry, and this rain was welcome, but frightening. Thunder grumbled and rumbled, and forks of lightning lit up the sky. Skipper whined at the door, and Nick let him in. I hoped my kittens were snug as a bug in a rug under the boards behind the woodpile. The rain was unrelenting, and the noise and the lightning went for a long time. Nick was trying to get an explanation of where thunder comes from. No one bothered to answer him, probably because we didn't know. Maggie said she was told it was God moving his furniture around in heaven.

Every once in a while, the two silver bells on the phone made a dinging sound, caused by the electrical charge from lightning racing along the phone wire to the house. That was a bit scary. Dad said we needed the rain, and I think most of us were awake off and on throughout the night as the rain continued to fall. In the morning, the grass looked greener, and everything looked like it had a soaking. There were puddles of water in the lane, which we hadn't seen for a long time!

As the hot weather continued, Roy and Will got a notion to sleep outside. The junkyard in the bush near the house abounded with old treasures. A bedstead was unearthed, complete with long rails to join the head and foot. Grass had grown through the rusty bedsprings, but encouraged by the resurrection of the old stove, the boys gave those bed pieces a once-over with the broom. They set it up in the small granary near the barn. Dad came up with a holey old mattress from somewhere, and they took their blankets and pillows from upstairs. Unfortunately, there was no hope to escape the mosquitoes that came in droves through the two gaping window spaces.

The first night they slept out there, I went to see how they were doing. The cool night air felt like heaven as I stepped out of the stuffy, hot house. When I looked in, all I could see were two lumps of blankets, as Roy and Will were completely covered. About that time, I heard the high whine of mosquitoes in my ear and I felt them in my hair.

"How is it, you guys?"

The boys answered me through their protection. "We can move your cot out here, Dot. It's so much cooler than in the house."

I slapped a mosquito that was burrowing into my cheek and squashed three more with one slap on my arm. "Maybe not. Goodnight!"

One morning, Fred Fiske came over and asked Dad if he could spare Roy for the day, as he needed help with fencing, His cows were getting out on the road, and it was high time to repair the fence and replace the old posts. Dad said, "Sure," and Roy hopped in Fiske's truck. My brother was growing up. He even looked different this summer, with a little mustache thing on his top lip. When he got home, he had a wide grin on his face. "I said no, but he gave me ten bucks for helping him."

I thought Dad would tie into Roy about taking money from a neighbor, but we all nearly fainted when Dad said, "You're an A-1 worker, Roy. Fred got a deal." Roy's hair had grown long, and that night he asked Dad to buzz it off with the clippers, as it was too hot in this heat.

It was on a Sunday night in August that we got to see another light show. Nick still talked about the northern lights and this time, it was another event in the heavens called the Perseid meteor shower. Miss Locken had told us to watch for it in August, particularly around the 12th, so we wrote it on the calendar. We didn't miss it. As darkness closed in late that night, we joined Roy and Will out in their granary bedroom. At about 11 o'clock, we stretched old blankets on the ground beside the granary. It was getting cool, and we covered up with more blankets from the house. Nick was eager, and so were we. Then it started! Almost all at once, we saw stars whizzing from one side of the sky, and then from the other. Sometimes they crisscrossed as they fell.

We were shouting, "There's one!"

"Oh, there's two!"

"Did you see *that*?!" And after a while, we were quiet, silently watching the magic. Clouds moved in after midnight and so we gathered up our covers and ourselves - Nick and I to the house, and Roy and Will to their summer bedroom.

One of our favorite songs in our Friday afternoon music at school was "Swinging on a Star". The little kids loved it because it was silly, about being a mule or a pig. Nick was getting very sleepy, but he was still buzzed up from seeing the falling stars, and we sang our way to the house.

Liz and her love for music had worn off on us. She remembered when songs were popular on the radio, and who sang them. This one was Bing Crosby from 1944, one year before I was born. The hundreds of shooting stars we had seen were still zipping through my mind. As I curled up on my cot, I lay awake, thinking. Not long ago, on the day Maggie and I visited Aunt Hazel's house in the city, I was wishing I could live in the city, but after the last while on the farm, I had a different attitude. I was a lot better off now than I had been a year ago. Our life was improving. I was still puzzled over Mom's death and the secrecy around it. When I was older, I would find out if it killed me.

The summer work was never ending. Maggie ordered cases of fruit that came in on the train from the Okanogan. She bought peaches, pears, plums and apricots, and the station master let us know by phone when they arrived. The different kinds of fruit didn't come at the same time, so we needed to be ready any day to can whatever fruit arrived. Canning was a colossal task, first carrying pails of water from the well and heating it on the outdoor cookstove in a boiler. We kept the water steaming, as we sterilized the jars, and prepared the fruit. The sealers took hours to "process" but as Maggie said, "We'll be happy we did it when we need something tasty in the winter." Rhubarb was easier to get. It grew in abundance in our sandy garden, and we canned it too, with one thin slice of banana on the top, inside each jar. Canning outside kept the heat and the mess out of the house. I gave Maggie credit for her brilliant idea of a summer kitchen.

Maggie looked worn out each evening. Her belly was puffing out, and I told her she should wear the smocks from Aunt Hazel rather than old baggy shirts of Dad's. After that, she wore a different one every day, and tied back her wild red hair with a ribbon. Maybe I was getting used to her looks, but she looked prettier than when Dad brought her home. Liz told me some women look way better when they are going to have a baby, and maybe that was working for Maggie. She said that she appreciated my help each day with the canning and the garden. It somehow didn't seem fair for her to do it alone. Liz had pushed the idea of everyone pitching in to help. "I'll tell you what, Dot, first we work together, and then we play together."

Maggie mentioned the time her mom came in the buggy, bringing the plants and the eggs. She placed a box on my cot and said, "I asked her to bring my books from home that time, so I could give them to you." I couldn't believe my ears. I hadn't read a book all summer, and I was starving for an inviting story. If these were even close to *An Old-Fashioned Girl*, I had some fine times ahead. I opened the box and looked inside. "Oh glory!" I stacked them up: *Little*

Women, Cheaper by the Dozen, The Long Winter, Anne of Avonlea, The Secret Garden, Heidi, and *Black Beauty.* I yelled, "Yes!" when I spied Thornton W. Burgess books in the bottom of the box. They were different titles than we had at school: *The Adventures of Buster Bear, Old Granny Fox,* and *The Adventures of Paddy the Beaver.* I could hardly wait to tell Nick. Our summer had just turned golden. I didn't know which book to start with, so I grabbed *The Secret Garden* and headed outside. I had a perfect shady spot in mind. On my way out, I stopped.

"Thanks Maggie!"

"You're welcome to them. My aunt gave me one every year when I was younger, but I'm not much of a reader."

We were all sitting at the table when there was a long, very long, ring on the phone. Maggie hurried, as much as she could hurry with her growing belly, and picked up the receiver. She listened, didn't say hello, and then hung the receiver back on the hook. She was used to having a phone before she came to our place and as she explained later, that was a general ring. It was how the operator relayed messages to the community. Now that we had a phone we would know what was going on. This general ring announced a show, *Ma and Pa Kettle at the Farm,* at the McKeen community hall on Friday night.

Dad surprised us by saying, "Well, let's go." I shouldn't say he surprised us. I should say he *shocked* us. We wondered what was going on. Dad, taking his family out for a special treat? Hardly possible, but it happened. We got spruced up on Friday after an early supper, and off we went, us kids pummeled by the wind in the back of the truck, Dad, Maggie and Mac in the front.

The big hall was packed with people sitting on rows of wooden chairs. Ma and Pa Kettle had fifteen kids and the show was so funny, everybody laughed their heads off. Ma Kettle's prized speckled hen spent her time strutting across the kitchen table and laying eggs in Pa Kettle's hat. I knew we would laugh about it for weeks to come.

If we hadn't got the phone, we wouldn't have heard about the show. I thought back to the day Nick was so sick, and Dad had to drive somewhere to call the doctor. Having the phone now was going to be very practical.

The garden was growing, and so were the weeds. One morning before the sun got too hot, Maggie and I decided to thin the carrots, so the remaining ones could grow bigger. We pulled a pail full of bright orange, baby carrots. They tasted sweet, and nothing like the carrots in the cellar during winter. These were like candy. We washed them all, and cut off the tops. I tied a nice bunch of them with a red piece of string, and put them in Mrs. Fiske's empty cake pan. I remembered another lesson from Liz. "I'll tell you what Dot, never return a cake pan without putting something in it. That shows you're a good neighbor." I explained it to Maggie. She had never heard of doing that, but she agreed it was the right thing to do. That night, Dad and Maggie went for a short drive in the truck to the Fiske farm a mile away, to return the pan and the carrots. I was proud that I remembered some of the things Liz taught me, and I hoped she would be proud of me, too.

NOW I KNOW

ater that week, Aunt Hazel arrived on a special mission. She drove into the yard unannounced in her old brown Plymouth, the one we rode in to see Liz. She gave us all kinds of compliments about our summer kitchen. I was glad that Maggie had spread out a red, checkered cloth on the table that morning. I got out of bed early to have some time outside before the wind started up, and as I walked in the pasture, I couldn't resist picking a bunch of yellow buffalo beans. When I got back to the house, Maggie put them in some water in a sealer and said they looked so nice, we should go all out and find a tablecloth.

Aunt Hazel complimented Maggie on how nice she looked in the smock she had loaned her. Nick and Mac came running when our aunt called them, and their eyes bugged out when she put a bag of store bought cookies on the table. Of course, Roy and Will missed out. They were out in the field making hay with dad which was a hard and hot job under the fiery August sun.

My aunt promised the boys she would be back with something else for them, and motioned me to follow her down the lane. We walked towards the school, and she talked so much, I thought we might get the whole distance to the school gate before she suggested we turn back. We sat down on the grass, close to the fence, at the same place I stopped on the last day of school. She pulled an envelope out of her dress side pocket.

"I brought something for you, Dot. I've been thinking of you ever since you came that day to see Liz. I looked through some old things, because I had saved this letter, but didn't know for sure where it was."

"Read it to me," I said, as I closed my eyes. I was sure it had to do with Mom. I lay on my back on the prickly grass, letting the sun warm my face.

"It's a letter to me from your Mom, from the hospital when you were born."

I didn't move. I could hardly wait, but I didn't say a word.

"Dear sister Hazel,

Well here I am in the hospital, and it is all over. I have my baby girl, and I can't tell you how happy I am. I'm going to name her Dorothy after our mom. I hope you like that, and if you have a girl sometime, I hope you don't mind that I have already taken the name. She is so tiny and so cute. I thank the Lord above for this precious gift. Robert came to see her yesterday when he heard on the hospital bulletin that she was born. He says we will have to get used to having a girl. We might be home on Saturday, if all goes well. I wanted to drop you a line and tell you that I'm so happy.

As ever, Violet."

I was so choked up I couldn't speak. My aunt said, "I am giving you this letter, Dot. You should have it. I also brought these pictures."

There were five photos - one of Mom and Hazel when they were toddlers wearing hand-knitted dresses; another of Grandma Dorothy, the one I was named after; then a picture of the two sisters, Violet and Hazel as teenagers; and another was the same wedding photo I had found in Mom's trunk. The last photo Hazel had taken of us—Mom, Dad, Roy, Will, and tiny baby me - our family as it was at that time, in 1946.

"You can have these, Dot. I'm sure your brothers will want to see them, too. There is one more thing. It's in my car. Your mom and I shared a doll when we were little girls. It's for you."

I remembered the Esmond bunny doll blanket back at the house that Liz had teased me about. The doll would be wrapped in the blanket and safely kept in my mom's trunk.

I wondered if I dared wreck this perfectly wonderful time with my aunt. I decided to go for it.

"Aunt Hazel, did Dad kill my mom?"

My aunt had been holding back tears throughout the reading of the letter, and our time together. At my question, she burst out crying, "Oh Dottie, is that what you've been thinking all this time?" I nodded.

"No, no, no, no-!! He didn't! No one killed her. Why on earth do you think that?"

"Because no one will talk about it. People don't just die, Auntie, not a healthy woman like my mom. She wasn't old. She wasn't sick."

Aunt Hazel looked in the distance. "It's hard to talk about. I miss her so much. I know you do, too, Dot."

I instantly thought of the blood on the sheets. Could it be that my aunt did not know why her sister died? I felt strong and ready to stand up for my rights.

"I'll find out even if you won't tell me. I will find out why she died."

I was still stretched out on the ground, and even though she was wearing a light-colored dress, my aunt lay down beside me. We looked up at the puffy clouds.

"Your mom and I were like twins. We did everything together. We used to lie outside in the summer, like this, and watch the cloud shapes turn into animals or people."

I didn't say anything.

"Violet had a miscarriage, Dot. That's when something goes wrong when you're pregnant and there's not going to be a baby. It's all over."

Liz had told me a lot of things, but she had never mentioned the word "miscarriage".

"Is there blood?"

"Yes, Dot there was. Your Dad was working in the field, and he didn't come in till noon. By then she had lost too much blood. She had passed away."

"Alone?"

"Yes, alone. Your dad was heartbroken. He blamed himself."

I thought of all those weeks and months when I had blamed him, too. I thought of the time I had said, "People can die in this house and nobody cares." I felt mean and small.

"You should have told us, Aunt Hazel."

"I know." We stood to our feet, my aunt wrapped me in her arms and we both cried. Fiske's truck rattled by on the road. We hardly noticed. So now I had the truth at last. No one killed her. We just had rotten luck, that day last June, when we lost the best mother in the world.

MY LIFE LESSONS

September and October 1956

As summer turned to fall once again, we settled back into Briar Rose School, all set for a fresh start. My Grade 6 reader, *All Sails Set,* with the ship and the gull on the green cover, was already familiar to me. As I leafed through the pages, I recognized every story and every poem from listening in to former Grade 6 students. There would be lots for me to learn in the coming year, and the blank unmarked notebooks and new pencils renewed my determination to do quality, neat work.

Miss Locken handed out spelling words for all of us to work on as she had scheduled a spelling bee for the whole school in the afternoon. At noon hour, we were frantically reviewing the word list for our grade, as we were rusty from being out of school all summer.

The same day, Miss Locken told us she planned to be married at the end of the school year, in July, 1957. She had asked Mr. Turner's permission to introduce her fiancé to us when he came to pick her up and drive her to her parents' house in town for the weekend. David was tall, dark and handsome, sort of a cowboy type. I could tell Louise and Edith were eyeing him up and thinking Miss Locken had found herself a prize! Roy raised his hand, "Miss Locken, I have a question for David."

Our teacher nodded, and Roy said with a sly grin, "David, she told us all about Leap Year and Sadie Hawkins. Did *she* propose to *you*?

Her boyfriend burst out laughing, and Miss Locken's face went beet red. "No," he answered, "It was me who did the asking, and I had to beg!"

The plan was that after the spelling bee, we would finish the week with music class. David took his guitar out of the case, sat on a chair beside Miss Locken's desk, and they began to sing, "In the Blue Canadian Rockies". I think I fell in love with him then and there! My dreams of travel and seeing the world had not gone away, and hearing the song about the Rockies renewed my hopes. Nicky looked across the rows of desks at me, and I winked at him. That train whistle was still calling our names.

Looking ahead, I was well aware winter would come again, as well as the Christmas plays, long rides in the cutter, and maybe another wicked three-day blizzard. We had all moved up to the next grade. Roy was now 15, Will 13, me 11, Nicky 7, and Mac 4. The next main event was coming up in a week or two. The baby would change everything.

Another monumental change was Dad's purchase of a TV! Other families had one and we were wishing, but we certainly weren't counting on having one in our house anytime soon. Roy and Will had seen a TV a couple of times in Fletcher's Store in McKeen. I saw a TV at the Fiske's. It had a small screen, and was sitting on the buffet in their living room. They invited us over one Sunday night to watch *Father Knows Best*. It was like seeing *Ma and Pa Kettle* at the hall that time, but now we could see a show right in Fiske's house!

When we came home from school on Nick's birthday, October 29th, there it was! A sleek, black TV installed in our living room where we could see it from the table. On the screen was a red-haired puppet with freckles named Howdy Doody, and Mac was giggling his head off. That night we watched *I Love Lucy* and the whole family laughed at how crazy she acted. Lucille Ball was the star's name, and she was proud of her red hair. What was it with all these redheads?! Probably the baby would have red hair, too!

One Saturday afternoon while Maggie worked in the kitchen, I sat on my cot with a pencil and my notebook from Liz. I skimmed over the recipes she had written there for me, and the words to some of our favorite songs.

At the top of a fresh page I wrote: **Lessons I Have Learned.**

I wrote my list. First, **Love is better than hate.** I started thinking of that one the day I went to see Liz at the hospital, and she told me I had to stop hating Dad. She had given me the best possible advice. She was so right, love is better than hate. Maybe Dad and I could get to the love part someday. I could still see him lying on the couch that time when I told him Liz had been nicer to me in a few months than he had been in 11 years. That's when he said, "I figure to do better with that." I figured he was doing better.

My next lesson was **Tears are okay.** That one started with Aunt Hazel, on the same day of the visit to Liz. When Maggie said, "Dot's bawling,", it was Aunt Hazel who said "Tears are okay." I had been learning in the past year not to be ashamed of tears. Those were healing tears with Aunt Hazel when we cried for Mom on our recent walk on the road. You don't cry all the time, but sometimes, tears are okay.

Just a Dot. That was the lesson I learned over my salt and flour map of Canada. I am only a little dot on the prairie, but I make a difference because I am here. I am no better and no worse than anyone else! That one I would always hang on to.

You can't change the wind. That was Maggie's comment when I told her I wanted the annoying wind to stop! She was so right, I can't change the wind. Nor can I change that my Mom died, that Liz got sick, that Dad married Maggie. There are dozens of things I can't change, but I can accept what has happened, even if I don't like it. This fourth lesson made the most sense of all. I flipped to the front of my notebook. With no further explanation needed, I wrote in my best handwriting: "I cannot change the wind!"

Maggie had turned on the radio, and one of my favorite songs was playing. I listened to the tune and the words of "Moments to Remember" by the Four Lads. So many life-changing events had happened in the last year and a half. Some memories were good, some were bad, but all of them were mine to keep.

ACKNOWLEDGEMENTS

Thanks and love to the best siblings in the world:

- Trudy, my very own "Miss Locken" who carried me from her teacherage to the one room school.
- Sharon, my loyal sister who stood up to the teacher for knuckling me on the head.
- Jon, my brother who stood barefoot with me in the lane and still holds my hand.
- Le, my brother who listened as eagerly to my made-up stories as I did to his singing.
- Shelley, my youngest Sis, who is my friend for life.

Thank you to Lantern Hill Communications, for editing and proofreading.

Thank you to Edna Alford, for editing advice, enthusiasm and encouragement.

Thank you to my cheerleaders: Sunny, Teddi, Erin, Eden and Johanna.

Songs in the Public Domain
Count Your Blessings, 1897, Johnson Oatman

Poetry in the Public Doman
New Year's Morning, Helen Hunt Jackson
Quote from the Bible, John 14:2a, King James Version
September, Helen Hunt Jackson
Travel, Edna St. Vincent Millay

Just around the corner...

Many readers who read Dot on the Prairie, have asked the question, "But what happened to Liz?"
The answer is found in a brand new book titled:

Sure as the River

It is Liz's story of the unexpected twists and turns in her life which includes the hospital for the mentally ill and a home for unwed mothers. Her strength and determination inspire us to never give up. Hope is what we cling to - it is the one thing that is *as sure as the river*.

Wander Back to Saskatchewan Trilogy

By Charlotte Evelyn Sloan

Dot on the Prairie

Sure as the River

Something to Say